HOW TO KEEP ROMANCE IN YOUR MARRIAGE does away with the fancies and looks at the facts. It points out the dangers and steers married couples, young and old alike, past them toward a richer, more romanceful married life.

This is that rare book, a popular treatment of a subject too often cloaked in textbook language. It's a book for marriage counselors, for ministers, but most of all, for *anyone* who's married.

WILLIAM CLARK ELLZEY

Teacher, lecturer, marriage counselor, camp director, writer, minister, Red Cross worker, one-time deputy sheriff—the career of William Clark Ellzey has been as interesting as it has been varied.

Mr. Ellzey is a veteran marriage counselor and teacher, and is on the Marriage Education staff at Stephens College in Columbia, Missouri. As an ordained minister he is a member of the Methodist National Committee on the Family, and the Board of Managers of the Joint Department of Family Life, National Council of Churches. He has held officer responsibility in the National Council on Family Relations, and a committee chairmanship in the American Association of Marriage C

During World Wa as a Field Director f Cross in two Germ camps, an R.A.F. P and with the U.S. A and has three childr

HOW TO KEEP ROMANCE
IN YOUR MARRIAGE

HOW TO

KEEP ROMANCE

IN YOUR

MARRIAGE

BY

W. Clark Ellzey

Stephens College
Columbia, Missouri

ASSOCIATION PRESS

NEW YORK

Printed in the United States of America
American Book–Stratford Press, Inc., New York

FOREWORD

It is taken for granted that any couple looking forward to marriage must experience romance. That married people in general should enjoy it, is not so widespread an expectation. This book is written as a positive assertion that romance can be kept alive, and may become more powerful and meaningful through the years of marriage than it was before the wedding. Not everything involved in romance in marriage is to be found in these pages, but there are some suggestions as to why it may not be present in marriage, and what to do to create it and cause it to grow.

My own experience of romance in marriage has been enriched by the privilege of looking behind the scenes into the lives of others who have invited me to share or help. Whatever insights this book may reveal, therefore, are derived from glimpses into that sacred private world of lonely struggle behind the "front" which each of us puts up before the world outside of ourselves. I have seen agony and ecstasy, cowardice and heroism, and I walk the royal road of romance in marriage with such gladness and humility as comes from the many opportunities which I have had to lend a hand.

Many people, probably very much like yourself, have really written this book. I have only put the

97

words and thoughts together. Among those who have
contributed are the members of the families in
which I am son and son-in-law, brother and brother-
in-law, and the families in which I am husband,
father, father-in-law, and grandfather. But many
more people than these have had a hand in this enterprise. They are my memorable teachers, my estimable
colleagues, friends, and lovable enemies, my provoca-
tive students, and the many people not unlike yourself whom I have come to know through twenty-five
years of personal and group counseling. Many of
them have urged that I put down in book form some
of the things which we talked over together. I hope
that it may prove a useful instrument to minister,
marriage counselor, professional therapist, and parents and friends of the newly married, and that it
pleases them and encourages or challenges you, or
suggests a way for you to realize that portion of your
dreams of romance which is possible of human
achievement in marriage.

                                        W. CLARK ELLZEY

CONTENTS

CHAPTER ONE

Romantic Illusion and Romance

Romance is as old as the human race. Follow the explorers into caves that have been closed for thousands of years. Flash a light on the damp walls and examine the symbols, faintly scratched there, which represent the earliest records of man. You may discover in picture story the silent watch of the "he," the sudden rush in the night, the startled cry of the "she," and only an ancient moon to witness the primeval drama. Dig up the ruins of ancient civilizations and look at the evidence of the thrills of the chase, the fury of battle, the quest for love, and all the wild excitement in the adventure of life. Open the doors of tombs, translate the tablets of clay, follow the dim lines on old skins, the marks on ragged papyri. Read the faded words on manuscripts yellow with age. The story is ever the same: the search of a man for a maid, a lullaby in the night, the struggle to protect and provide, and the longing to know in the great unknown.

When you discover romance in history it seems to masquerade because it wears the clothes of time and place. It speaks the language of geography and race. It appears in the royal robes of kings and queens, the apparel of merchants, and the humble garments of peasants. It stalks the trails of the caravans and rides in the contest arena. The voice of romance can be heard in whispers among the shadows and in the husky shouts of the day. Its image is seen in eyes that smile and dare. It speaks in the rapture of ecstacy, the protest of pain, the joy of laughter, and the harsh dry gasp of despair. Romance gives life to history. It splashes color on the pages of scripture in every religion in the world.

Everyone is searching for romance. There is an audience for the teller of love stories, and thousands listen to the pulsing strains of the love song. Romance followed the path of fable and sang in the heart of the minstrel all across the ages; but at no time in history has romance had so great a gallery as today. It has top billing on radio, TV, stage, and screen. We are swamped with a flood of magazines and books which deliver romance secondhand. We must have romance, and if we do not have it to our satisfaction in real life, we will take it secondhand.

There Are Various Ideas About Romance

We have been taught by ancient love stories, suspenseful drama, and the miraculous movies to think of romance as the rainbow path toward marriage. When we are young we are encouraged to look forward to it with sparkling anticipation. When we are old we are reminded that we may look back on it with a warm glow of memories. We come to consider romance an event in life instead of a way of life which is different at different times in life, but there all the way through. We expect it to precede a wedding and to last at least as long as a honeymoon. We have seen it fade so many times thereafter that we have regarded its fading as inevitable.

We say to ourselves, and sometimes to newlyweds, Now you will have to settle down to the hard realities of life. Romance as we think of it does not cast a moonlit sheen around the daily grind of making the money to pay the bills. There is nothing romantic about washing dishes and scrubbing floors, except in the magazine advertisements. We want the kind of romance that characterized courtship to be there all the rest of our lives. We have so thoroughly identified romance with the love affair preceding marriage that we are blind to any other kind. We measure all romance by the premarital fragment. We prove it by the wonder and awe with which we point to the married couple who, after several years of marriage, attempt to prove they are still in love by acting toward each other as they did before they were married. This use of adolescent romance as the measure of all the romance in life would be amusing, if it were not so pathetic.

There is a kind of romance appropriate to each age and stage of growth. There is romance in babyhood, and romance for the childhood years. There is romance for the first new love, and romance for the mating time. There is romance for the maturing which has depth and breadth not possible for youth. And there is romance abounding in worth and meaning for the aging which only they can know and all too few ever experience. We predetermine our own disappointment when we expect the romance of one age to be present in all ages—or in any age except the one to which it is appropriate.

We cannot have the body of a person twenty-five and the body of a child of five at the same time. We can have the body of a twenty-five-year-old and the mind of a child of five, but only if the mind has been arrested in its development. Such a condition throws life out of gear. We can have the richness and full-ness of mental life on an adult level only if the mind grows up too. Body, mind, emotions—all parts of our life—are involved in our experience of romance. We might deliberately try to arrest the development of any part of us, or we might stop growth when we had no intention of doing it, but such could not happen without distorting life. The attempt to ex-perience romance characteristic of adolescence all the rest of the way through life is, in effect, an attempt to arrest love life on an adolescent level. If we do stop growth on this or any other level, we deny ourselves the possibilities of romance on any more mature level.

A movie star is quoted as saying that marriage kills romance. She has had three marriages which she offers as proof. Apparently marriage did kill for her the only kind of romance she knows anything about. The pattern is easily recognizable. Follow romance into marriage. Premarital romance is inappropriate to, and cannot stand, the demands of marriage—and it is soon gone. Marriage has killed romance. You must get out of the marriage and look for a new romance with someone else. When it leads to marriage and fades away, get out of that situation and do it all over again with another partner. Ministers, doctors, lawyers, and others called upon to give counsel to people who are unsatisfied with their marriage are frequently confronted with this limited and misleading concept of romance.

Romance Differs Before and After a Wedding

For most of us, our approach to marriage was probably quite romantic. If you look up the word "romantic" you may find something like "fanciful, unworldly, fabulous, imaginative, dreamy, impractically or frivolously idealistic." That is a good description of most of the world's so-called "great love stories." Those words probably describe the greater portion of the romance upon which we decided to get married. That is not to say that we were totally "out of this world" and utterly unaware of reality. It is to suggest that perhaps a major portion of our premarital romance was.

There are many good reasons why this may have been so. A part of premarital romance depends upon the blocking of sex. The highly imaginative aspects of desire and anticipation are enhanced by restraint, and inflated by being blocked. Society requires that the satisfaction of sex needs be restricted to marriage. No matter how far a couple may go toward satisfying them before marriage there is always the fascinating anticipation of possibilities within marriage. This part of the dream aspects of premarital romance is inevitable. For most couples approaching marriage it makes up a considerable portion of their romance.

Since we were not yet experiencing all the intimacies of living together, and saw each other most of the time at our near best, there was strong possibility that we gained an incomplete impression of each other, and that some of that impression we supplied out of our own imagination. Romantic love is conducive to dreams. We can see it more clearly now in looking back. The "girl of my dreams" is so wonderful precisely because she is fanciful and "out of this world." She is impractically and idealistically unreal. She exists and can exist only in a dream. You can revel in an imaginary romance with her, but when you seek romance with a real person there is not so much revel.

Some married people attached their dream to the person they married and had their romance with their dream, not the person they married. When they began to know the person they married, some preferred the real romance they were able to discover with the real person. Others resented the fact that their marriage partner turned out not to be their dream, and went looking for other people upon whom to attach a new dream.

Now look up the word "romance" in the dictionary and you will find something like "a long story of love." Some people would interpret it to mean that a couple were in love for a long time before they were married. The idea that "a long story of love" might include all the long years of marriage does not fit their conception of love or romance. Or they feel that the only kind of love or romance that is desirable is that which happens before marriage. The dictionary has other words with which to describe romance. It is "wonderful," "colorful," and it can be "thrilling" and "practical" at the same time. It is "adventurous" and "exciting" and very much in this world. All of these words apply more extensively to reality than to dreams.

Any of the words used in defining romance may be applied to the very real experience and adventure of achieving mutually satisfying sexual adjustment in our marriage. The words we select to describe that experience will depend upon the degree of our success in the achievement. When we discover maximum, mutually shared satisfaction in our married love, our resulting sex attitudes and feelings are considerably different from those we had prior to marriage. During courtship, abetted by romantic love making, we derived our greatest sex satisfactions from our imagination and dreams; now, in marriage, our desires are fulfilled in a repeated act of love which suffuses our entire personalities and enriches our husband-wife relationship. Meager achievement and unsatisfactory adjustment, however, can drive us to resort to our premarriage dream world of unrealized sexual longings.

Not only in sexual adjustment, but in all other relationships and experiences we have in marriage, living with a real person eliminates whatever aspects of premarital romance fail to fit the real experience. The fanciful evaporates, and with it the psychological and emotional responses to the unreal. If a couple are successful in adjusting to and fulfilling the needs of each other, their marriage may enable them to know romance that is real and priceless. It may have lingering whiffs of fancy and dream but these will not make up the major portion of their romance. The wonder of their companionship may be quite real, and thrilling. The building of a home in which love abounds and continues to grow may be adventuresome and exciting.

Apparently we cannot have at one and the same time that part of romance or that kind of romance which depends upon the blocking of sex, and that kind which depends upon the satisfactions of sex. Neither can we experience simultaneously the scintillating responses to the fantastically unreal and the thrilling satisfactions in our successful achievements with the real. Romance before marriage is not comparable to romance in marriage. If our only concept of romance is that which fits romance before marriage, we are doomed to marriage without romance. What we expect, therefore, has a lot to do with what we discover of romance in our marriage.

How Can We Find Romance in Marriage?

If we are not blocked from romance in marriage by the idea that a small fragment of romance—that which is experienced immediately before marriage—is the only romance there is, then we may go on toward achieving romance in our marriage. The royal road is not difficult to see. Traveling it successfully is another matter. Romance in marriage is to be found in the wonder of relationships that are colorful and thrilling. The romance of marriage is the excitement and adventure of mixing the fanciful world of imagination with the practical realities of married life so that dreams are not lost—nor are they mistaken for reality—or sought as a poor substitute. The romance of marriage is "a long story of love" which may include all the hazardous experiences throughout life. The romance of marriage is to be found through the achievement of success in marriage. We all want it. Why do so many of us fail to find it?

If we look into those marriages where people seem to be experiencing romance we may discover some clues. In such marriages people seem to have an unusually mature capacity to love. What is a mature capacity to love? Are there people who cannot love at all in ways which will make romance possible? How can you tell what kind of love you have and how mature it is? What can you do if you find that you must grow up in your love life before you can ever have romance in your marriage?

People seem to have reasonable expectations of themselves and each other in those marriages where romance is found. What are unreasonable expectations? In such marriages people seem to like their relatives, and apparently the feelings are mutual. What have relatives to do with romance? Can two persons experience romance in their marriage and not like their relatives? Some homes which look like palaces seem to vibrate with the loving laughter of romance, and in others, where people wallow in wealth, there is an echo of hollow mockery at the faintest suggestion of it. Romance can be found where home is a shack, but some shacks house people whose lives are utterly devoid of romance. Apparently it cannot be bought with any amount of money, and yet romance may be found where there is lavish abundance of wealth. It can be found where pennies are counted with care, but it is not always found among people who have little of this world's goods. If it does not depend upon having or not having money, what is the relation of money to romance in marriage?

In marriages where people feel the thrill of adventure and the excitement of achievement there would seem to be an increasingly satisfying sexual relationship. It appears to have gone far beyond the first physically dominated experiences of early marriage and blends with the spiritual in a wonder-filled and meaningful communion of personality. Adequate knowledge and healthful attitudes and feelings make possible discoveries in sexual experience otherwise impossible. What is adequate knowledge about sex? What is an unhealthy attitude or feeling about sex? How can sex life increase or destroy romance in marriage?

In marriages where people are experiencing romance, there would seem to be no great threat of the "eternal triangle." What safeguards can be developed against this age-old threat? In marriages where people have a zest for living and loving, people seem to have found out what freedom is all about, freedom in marriage. There is no hint of "the ball and chain." What is freedom in marriage and how does it differ from freedom out of marriage? How can you acquire it? How could you lose it?

Romance is never found in marriages of those who have never grown up. Immaturity destroys romance in marriage—and frequently marriage itself. What is immaturity? How can you recognize it in yourself or anyone else? What can you do about it? Some people with children lack any suggestion of romance, while others surrounded by them seem to possess an abundance. Some married couples with no children have rich experience of romance, while others have little or none. Is there a romance of parenthood? Do children need parents who have found romance in their marriage?

Look into those marriages in which the children have grown up and established homes of their own. Some people in these older marriages show a restlessness which may turn into illness of body or mind. Others seem to have fresh vitality with which to begin adventures into new freedoms, and excitement runs high. How can we find romance satisfying for the retirement years?

This book is written in the hope that it may help some of us who are engaged or married to clarify our expectations about romance in marriage; and also help us find a way to create or increase romance in our marriage. There is no guaranteed formula. But we could all know more than we do about ourselves and about others. We could know more about how to get along together. That is true no matter how much we already know. We might acquire a clearer idea about how good a marriage risk we are, to ourselves and to the person who married us. We might discover some little way in which to make our marriage more successful, no matter how successful it is now. We might discover some additional insights and understandings which would make it possible for us to experience more thrill and excitement in the adventure of our marriage, even when we did not think it possible.

Romantic Love and the Real Thing

About as many people seem to be victims of love as
there are those who are benefited by it. We expect
love to be beautiful and wonderful and blest with
rainbows. Our attitude suggests that we want it to
represent an ecstatic trance—which it does, now and
then—but love is also capable of warping and twist-
ing life. It can torture as well as soothe and comfort.
Love can save but it can also destroy. We have never
been quite so shocked as when our romantic sentimentalism about mother-love was shaken by proof
that some kinds of mother-love may be the most vicious influence imaginable in the life of a child.

There Is Great Need for Understanding

No word in the English language, with the possible
exception of the word "sex," covers quite so much
pain and confusion in human relationships as the
word "love." Nor is there any other word that refers
to such exciting and wonder-filled experience as that
which is possible with love at its best. Such a statement implies that love can also be at a worst. The

marriage counselor who has been invited behind the scenes in the lives of people for many years knows from observation that love has a "best" and a "worst." When love results in tragedy it is most likely because of our lack of knowledge about it, our careless mishandling, or our failure to grow up in our love life.

Some people are so enraptured by their romantic ideas about love that they resist any attempt to understand it lest such an effort might destroy it. If their love is flimsy to that extent a marriage is sure to destroy it. Some of us have trusted ideas about love which have proved to be untrue, but we shaped our expectations and made our decisions on the basis of our ideas, right or wrong. Some married people think that if their marriage is successful and love lasts, they are "lucky in love." If marriage proves somewhat unheavenly we are "victims of fate," we were fooled by an "infatuation," or "our love has grown cold," and it is all through no fault of our own, of course. The fact that our situation is the inevitable result of wrong ideas about love, is hard to understand.

One of the most dangerous assumptions about love is the idea that two persons who are in love should marry because they are in love. It is expressed most simply in the statement, "We married for love." Evidently we have never been told that it is quite possible to fall in love with a person with whom we cannot have a successful marriage. We look upon love as a sign that we should marry. We do not know that some people who get divorces are still in love with each other. Romance is not possible in a marriage where there is no love; on the other hand, romance may disappear quickly from that marriage where people assumed that love was all that was necessary and could be trusted as the only guide into marriage.

One of the most costly and mistaken ideas about love is the idea that love as we experience it before we are married and through the honeymoon should remain just as it was, all through life. Nobody would expect to love when he was twenty years old as he did when he was ten, but many of us seem to expect with childlike naïveté or desperate hope that we shall love all through the remaining years as we did at twenty. If a couple who are in their forties "bill and coo" like newlyweds we smile approvingly, sometimes with envy, and conclude that they are still in love. The idea that forty-year-old people might have ways of expressing their love which bring greater satisfactions than by imitating youngsters barely out of adolescence, does not seem to occur. Perhaps it is because most of our ideas about love are limited to the romantic love characteristic of adolescence. We must discover the nature of love as it matures if we are to have romance in our marriage.

Another tricky idea about love is that strong physical attraction is love. Sex has a part in love; but sex appeal is not, by itself, love at all. It is possible to feel the urgent tug of sex appeal from someone you could not love. Yet, some couples have responded to this attraction, misinterpreted as love, engaged in satisfying sex desire, and followed its intoxicating enticement into a marriage which became barren or could not last. It is not possible to know the wonder of romance in marriage to its fullest extent without the sexual expression of love, but it is also not possible to have a marriage, much less romance, on sex alone. When marriage has been entered with the feeling that sex was love, romance may still be found, however, if the other elements of love are recognized and developed.

It is generally recognized that divorce is not the sole measure of failure in marriage. Certainly legal termination of the relationship is evidence of failure, but many marriages which still exist on the books and behind respectable fronts do not exist so far as the people in them are concerned—or at best they are meager and fragmentary marriages. Romance is not in them. Prominent among these barren marriages are those entered with the false conception that physical attraction is love. Among those marriages filled with romance are some which were begun with this mistaken idea, but were salvaged because the marriage partners were willing to learn and found the way to add to the quality of their love the other elements which make for romance.

Will We Love Only One Person Forever?

We recognize that it is possible and normal for us to fall in love with several persons before we choose a husband or a wife. It disturbs us greatly, however, if someone suggests that we could be in love with two persons at the same time. We attempt to safeguard our romantic idea by avowing that one of the relationships must be infatuation, because only one could be the "real thing." Yet loving two persons at the same time is not an uncommon experience. We love our father and mother at the same time. We do not love them exactly alike, but we love them very really in both cases.

Our romantic idea is related to the false conclusion that love means a marriage should occur, and it annoys us because we do not believe in two marriages existing at the same time, no matter how many we may have, one after another. To believe that you must love only one person at a time, yet to find yourself in love with two persons is somewhat confusing. However disturbing such a predicament before a wedding, it is devastating if it occurs afterward. We do not know that it is quite possible to fall in love with someone besides our husband or wife somewhere along through marriage and still be in love with our marriage partner. We do not think that it should happen, therefore we conclude that there is something terribly wrong if it does.

The all-important fact is not that you have fallen

in love before or after a wedding, with one or a dozen people, but *what you do about it!* If you understand that it does not mean that your marriage is all wrong, if you do not interpret it to mean that responsibilities and commitments made during the wedding are no longer in force, if you understand that being in love does not justify infidelity or adultery, then you do not need to be stampeded into destroying your marriage or greatly endangering your romance. If you have the romantic idea that love justifies anything, then romantic love may destroy romance.

The married person who seems to be tangled among the golden threads of too many loves need only examine his preconceptions about love with someone who knows, and make sure that only that love wherein life's investments are made is cultivated and developed. Other loves may come and go with little threat to one who understands that this is possible, but who does not think that each love must have complete and abandoned response merely because it invites it. That love which is nourished will grow.

Romantic love can make a couple feel that love will solve all problems, even finances. It may provide motivations for working toward solutions, but love will not make an unwise spender a skillful buyer. Marriage depends upon the sort of people who enter it. We took into our marriages whatever kinds of skills and abilities, strengths and weaknesses we had when we said, "I do." We could be very much in love and yet have ideas about life and marriage which would lead us into terrible arguments. With romantic love we merely argue and make up. With more mature love we work at the causes of our arguments and make those adjustments which contribute toward romance in marriage.

Among the illusions of romantic love is the idea that somewhere each of us has a "soul mate" who is the only person in the world with whom we can have romance in marriage. The fact is that we could marry and find happiness with any one of at least a thousand different persons. It is just as true that there are at least that many with whom we could not. Successful marriage—and happiness which derives from it—depends upon a good selection and fair achievement in making those adjustments required by the differences brought to the marriage by the man and woman who enter it. There is nothing fatalistic or accidental about it. Marriages may be "made in heaven" but they are actually built down here on earth out of human resources usually a little short of heavenly. The "soul mate" is possible only in the phantom imagery of imagination; it is a flimsy illusion of romantic love. Romance is discovered by people who keep trying to make themselves more lovable people and who know that their marriage is in their own hands.

There are many heated arguments over the question whether love at first sight is possible. A couple are attracted from the moment they meet. They go together and their love grows. They look back, and it seems that love was there from the very beginning. Some of it was, but not the love they have now. Another couple are caught in the flash flood of a terrific romantic love which passes quickly. In looking back they say that it could not have been love because it faded. That is like saying that a flower, torn out by its roots or starving for water, was not a flower because it faded. Examination will show that many of the same elements were in the love of the couple in whose relationship it continued to grow, as were in the love of the couple in whose relationship it faded out. Some of the elements of love were in both experiences from the start. Certainly not the sort of love with which it is safe to enter marriage is possible at first sight.

Romantic love is easily recognized because it usually sweeps people off their feet. It is very demanding, and causes people to brush aside any thought for the future which might interfere with its demands' being met in the present. It is impatient with any interference and it will not tolerate postponement of its desires. It rejects the idea that the future could be sold out in behalf of the present; or it persuades its victims to go ahead and sell, to let the future take care of itself. Romantic love causes people to feel that it will last forever just as it is at the moment. It gives rise to the statement that one can never love anyone else in the world and that if love is not satisfied, it will take many years or a life-

time to get over it. It attempts to coerce even love
itself when thwarted, or threatens dire consequences
even to the point of self-destruction. Romance is not
possible in marriage with such romantic love. Married people who have it, however, or must live with
it, may strive toward continued growth of love, toward sufficient maturity to eliminate these romantic
threats and create the real romance of marriage.

What Is Love?

No electrical engineer knows just what electricity is,
but he does know how it functions. That knowledge
enables him to work wonders with it. Maybe we can
never know exactly what love is, but we can learn a
great deal about how it functions. If we knew as
much about how love functions as the electrical engineer knows about how electricity functions we
might be able to work wonders in human relationships, even more amazing and thrilling than anything
ever done with electricity.

If we consider the ways in which we speak of love
we are caught in swirls of confusion. We "love
mother and father." We "love brother or sister." We
"love cats and dogs." We "love horses" and "peaches
and cream"; and we "love to fly." When a woman
stands fascinated in front of a window full of hats
and exclaims excitedly, "I love that hat," she is likely
to buy it. When she shows it to her husband he is
not so likely to use the word "love" in expressing his
opinion. But that same husband may "love golf," or

"love to fish," whereas his wife would use some other word for it. Apparently we shall have to look further than the way we talk about love to understand how it functions.

One of the earlier attempts to disclose the nature of love at its best is preserved for us in a letter written by a man many years ago. He said in his letter that there were certainly values in being able to express oneself in many languages and with a manner of speaking that might be most impressive, but that unless such a person expressed love in all that he was, as well as in what he was saying, it might be just so much noise. He said that a person who expressed love on a mature level seemed to be able to stand a lot of pain and still be kind to people around him. He did not say whether he meant physical or mental pain or both. The point is that a person who loves maturely will be able to think of others in spite of his pain, and show his love in being kind. Romance is found in marriage where people have that sort of love.

The writer pointed out how true love acts. He said that a person who loves does not think he is better than everybody else. He does not try to get attention and admiration by breaking all the rules. He does not stop with making people happy as he goes along but will go out of his way to make them happy. Romance will be in any marriage where a husband and a wife have that kind of love. The letter states that a person who really loves will not go around with a chip on his shoulder daring anybody to knock it off. Such a person is not easily offended either. He does not always watch to see if his mate is coming halfway. He does not get angry at just any little thing. The person who really loves, says the letter, will not be afraid and suspicious all the time. He can trust and he does trust. Even when things are bad he does not suspect the worst. He is not the sort of person who feels glad when somebody else is unhappy. He would probably feel best when people are enjoying life most, especially if he had anything to do with making their life more enjoyable.

That old letter is quite a letter. You can see what a love like that would do in any marriage. You can see how it would contribute toward romance in marriage. But the letter goes on to say that the person who loves can take it when things get bad, and he can take it for quite a while. The person with such love thinks that people are really very fine folk when you get to know them, and he brings out the best in them because he thinks that way. He is not a blind optimist, but he is no wailing pessimist. He hopes for the best, gets ready to deal with the worst if he has to, and takes whatever comes with a smile. And he will still be trying to help after everybody else has quit.

If you want to read this letter for yourself go to that library most people call the Bible and look among those books known as the New Testament; you will find the letter under the title of "First Corinthians." The letter has been divided into chap-

ters and verses for the convenience of those who cop-
ied it before we had the printing press, and you will
find in the thirteenth chapter what is said about love.
A man by the name of Paul wrote it to some people
he knew in the old country near a place called
Corinth.

Love Is Made Up of Elements

Modern psychologists point out that there are different kinds of love and that they are different because
they have different elements in them, or some elements developed to different degrees. For instance,
admiration may be in the love we have for our
father and it may be in the love we have for our
mother, but it is not exactly the same in both cases.
It may be in our love for a boy-friend or girl-friend,
or a husband or wife, and though it is admiration it
is not altogether of the same quality nor of the same
amount. We could admire someone we had just met.
If we kept up the acquaintance, became attracted,
fell in love and married, and then looked back from
a golden wedding anniversary we might see the silver thread of admiration running all the way back to
our first meeting. The thread would be of greater
texture and strength six months after our meeting
than at the very beginning, and it would be quite a
strand after fifty years of marriage. That is true if
admiration remained a part of our love and grew
as our acquaintance and experience filled it with
strength and meaning. But there are other elements

in love: hope and desire, sex and pride, thoughtfulness and reverence, respect and humility, and many others. If those elements and others like them are interwoven through marriage relationships they will provide the "ties that bind" and help to hold a marriage together. They might be woven into quite a beautiful pattern of romance.

Love, however, as the psychologist reminds us, has other elements in it of less attractive nature. Among the very desirable elements in anyone's love may be such undesirable ones as intolerance and deceit, false pride and selfishness, greed and the willingness to exploit even the loved one. In real life such elements as pleasure and pain, compliment and complaint, pride and humiliation, sacrifice and selfishness, and happiness and misery seem to get all mixed up together. It is like a clear stream into which mud is introduced. It becomes a different stream because of the elements which make it up.

Some of the elements can be present when two persons meet, but most of those elements which are present at first need to become much stronger before they think of marriage. Most of the elements in a love with which it is safe to approach marriage must have time in which to grow. Occasionally a few elements develop quickly and grow big, and a couple can be fooled into thinking that this is "it." The love which can stand the strains of the years, however, must have a great many of the positive and constructive elements of human relationships in it.

If it has too many of the destructive elements in it such as temper, dishonesty, untrustworthiness, jealousy, criticism, and abuse they may overwhelm the constructive elements and destroy them. If that happens, a marriage can sicken and romance can die.

Since no love on earth is perfect, all of us will have both supportive and threatening elements in our love for anybody. The important thing is to be able to recognize those which are supportive and to exercise them, so that they will grow and strengthen our love, and contribute to romance.

The Development of Love

When we were born everything in the universe existed for our special benefit as far as we were concerned. We wanted whatever made us feel good and we made a fuss over whatever made us feel bad. Since mother became associated with the pleasurable and seemed to be the cause of so much of it, we began to respond to her with pleasure. As father made his contribution in ways we could recognize, we made our response to him. But everything had to come our way; we could love no other way. Our infantile love was extremely self-centered. It had to be—we were so small in such a big world! We needed size and strength and self-assurance. Even with our love, we needed to get in order to grow. We were terribly frightened by anything which threatened to take mother, the most important source of our getting, away from us. We had to possess completely and it made us afraid and very angry when anything threatened our possession. Fear of losing and anger are the main elements of jealousy at any age. Jealousy is a sign of love that has not grown up, if it is present in the experience of an adult to a miserable degree. It is normal in the love of childhood and of early adolescence. Marriage requires more than childhood resources: it is an adult experience and requires adult resources. Romance cannot develop in that marriage where childish love threatens, until and unless that love is helped toward maturity.

Brothers and sisters were threats to our possession of mother and father. We had to learn to love them, and if our parents gave us enough love to reassure us we could love them in time. The other children in the neighborhood began to come within the horizon of our love but they had to come our way. When puberty arrived, and our sex glands began to supply hormones to our blood stream, our whole life began to change. It was most noticeable in our bodies. But we began to take different attitudes toward each other, and sometimes parents began to worry because their little boy had suddenly become "girl crazy," or their little girl was "boy crazy."

Love at this stage was pretty broad and inclusive, taking in whomever it settled upon for its own sake, but shifting easily and quickly. As we grew, the attachment began to last longer, but our love was still self-centered. We did not love the other person except as an instrument to satisfy our own love needs.

We had to have assurance of our desirability. Our ideas and feelings about ourself depended upon what others thought of us. Our need for popularity was great because our need for self-regard was great. If a person toward whom we were attracted gave us sufficient attention and responded in kind to our demanding love we were reassured. If we had enough of this experience during adolescence we gained sufficient self-confidence to enable us to be less demanding in our love. Toward the end of adolescence we could now and then love someone for his sake as much as our own. Occasionally we might love someone entirely for his sake. Our love was maturing from the long years of childish self-centeredness toward other-centeredness which is required for successful marriage.

We were achieving sufficient growth in our love life to be able to give, instead of having to get all the time. We were approaching the time when we could contribute toward the fulfillment of the needs of the loved one out of the strength and development of our own growing resources. Our satisfaction now came through our giving, not demanding and getting. When two persons who have grown up to this extent in their love life enter marriage, romance is all but inevitable. Some people, however, marry when one or the other has not yet grown up sufficiently and their love makes romance difficult if not impossible. When married people recognize at what stage their love is in the maturation process and

strive to develop it if it needs further growth, they
are very likely to find that their marriage is happier
than otherwise it would be. Some married people
have read books dealing with the growth and development of the emotions and have secured help from
them. Others have found guidance through talking
with some competent counselor who was able to help
them see where they were in their love life and what
to do about inducing further growth. Marriage, successful enough to make real romance possible, requires love that has grown beyond its adolescent
stage.

A young woman received a telegram from her
fiancé urging her to drop out of the university, rush
to a military base, and marry him. He had three days
before he was to be sent away, and there was a good
chance that he might be overseas for two or three
years. She loved him, and her first impulse was to
comply; but the more she thought about it the more
she questioned the wisdom of it. She found herself
examining the nature of their love for each other
when she went to talk it over with a long-time friend
of the family. She began to be aware that at no time
since she had known her fiancé had he seemed very
much concerned about what any decision might
mean to her. He always assumed that she would want
to do whatever he wanted to do; in fact, she could
have no other desire if she really loved him. Apparently she did not matter except as an instrument to
satisfy his love needs, and his ego made him assume

that such action on her part would satisfy her own. When she sent him a night letter pointing out the meaning of such a decision as it would affect her and their future, he sent her an ultimatum demanding that she come immediately or he would never marry her. She broke the engagement and felt considerably relieved.

When a person finds himself in a marriage with another whose love life must continue to grow to become other-centered, understanding and patience are the miracle workers. One cannot recognize a need for further growth and achieve growth merely through that recognition. It is not achieved through wishful thinking. It will have to result from one's working toward it over a period of time. A partner who understands and is patient is priceless. The more mature one may contribute most by giving an abundance of love in all the little ways through which mature love expresses itself. The other partner may be surprised at what happens if the positive elements of love are exercised through deliberate conscious practice. It is no mystery when a person who practices being thoughtful becomes a thoughtful person. Admiration, respect, compliments, encouragement, all the other positive elements of love, if practiced will contribute toward the development of a more lovable person. Such a person will be able to love more satisfyingly within the requirements of marriage. Love creates romance in marriage when people love that way.

A young man sat down in a marriage counselor's office and counted off his wife's faults on his fingers. He ended by asking the counselor whether he could see any way in which his wife was trying to make him happy. When the counselor asked if he had given his wife flowers or candy, or taken her places before they married, the young man replied that he had. When the counselor asked him why, he was surprised. The counselor explained that he might have done these things as a means of getting her for his wife, in which case he might not have ever loved her, just himself, and might have taken her only to satisfy a self-centered love. Or, he might have loved her before they were married and done those things to make her happy. The counselor pointed out that the young husband's question indicated his present love to be self-centered. If he had listed his own faults and asked himself what he was doing to make her happy it might have indicated an other-centered love. In that case he would not have come to the counselor, or if he did it would have been for help, not for justification and complaint.

The young man saw it and left the counselor's office with a conscious determination to work at the little matter of making his wife happy. His wife was amazed at the change in him, quite unable to account for it, but most responsive to it. There is no question about romance in their marriage.

The marriage counselor mentioned the incident above in making an address and was followed to his automobile by a man from the audience. The man said that he had just realized what was happening in his marriage. He said that his wife was "crazy about toy dogs" made out of wood, porcelain, iron, or whatever. He could not understand why she liked them so much. They were stuck around everywhere and, according to him, good for nothing but to gather dust. She used one big iron one for a door stop and he had "busted" his shin on it many times. That did not help his attitude toward her hobby, but he was always looking for some new dog to add to her collection. It did not matter where he found it—toy shop, dime store, gift shop, or drugstore. She always went into ecstasies over it when he gave it to her.

He then related how his wife would surprise him with some gadget which he could use in playing golf, or fishing or hunting. She did not see why he was so interested in these things, but every now and then she would come up with something he could use. It did not happen just on birthdays, or any special time. He concluded with the observation that it seemed each of them was trying to make the other one happy by getting something the other liked. He was a living picture of a husband who knew something about romance. It was in his eyes as he smiled, and in the tone of his voice when he talked about his wife.

The marriage counselor became acquainted with his wife and came to know some of their friends. He found that those friends were impressed by the way the man talked about his wife after eight years of marriage. They said that his wife was always bragging about her husband when they were both among friends. It was clear to all that these two loved each other. The husband expressed his pride in his wife's accomplishments in the community and encouraged her in whatever enterprises she undertook. That kind of love comes as near to guaranteeing romance in marriage as anything can.

It has been said that "a beautiful woman at twenty is an accident of nature, but a beautiful woman at forty is an achievement in living." If she is a married woman a part of her beauty is due to her husband's achievement in loving. Most men love their wives only as much as they feel a need to love them, not nearly so much as their wives need loving. We have been so concerned with the satisfaction of our own needs for so long that it takes considerable practice to get good at sensing the needs of others. When a man's attention is fixed upon his wife as a person whose happiness he wants to enrich, he will try to become more and more sensitive to her needs. In addition to the complication of having thought of ourselves for so long, most of us tend to read our own thinking and feeling into others. We would like to have a wrist watch, therefore and most certainly, anybody would like to have one, especially the one we are most concerned about. Many a wife would rather hear her husband say that he loved her on some occasion in addition to his sexual approach, than have him give her a wrist watch.

Most wives encourage their husbands only as much as they feel a need to encourage them, not nearly so much as the average man needs encouraging. This has no reference to the constant nagging of some wives who attempt to force a husband to achieve what they think he should in fulfillment of their own ambitions instead of his. It refers to the fact that every man in his struggle with the world at large needs the sort of belief in him and encouragement from his wife that will support his confidence in himself. If she loves him and believes in him and shows it in public as well as in private he can usually "whip the world," no matter what kind of world he is battling.

This deliberate effort on the part of each to sense the needs of the other in all relationships and experiences, this attitude that gropes to understand the meaning of life for the other, this constant searching for little ways in which to make life easier and happier for the other can make a very lovable person, as well as a person capable of loving very unusually. Anyone who has become that sort of person seems somewhat embarrassed if someone remarks about it, and somewhat surprised.

There was a time when we had to pay attention to each step as we were learning how to walk. We kept on practicing and soon we were able to go anywhere without paying particular attention to our walking. Love which is grown up enough for romance in marriage is like that. We have to give conscious attention to sensing the other person's needs and extending ourself beyond our own needs to meet them. We may not be too good at it at first, but we become more skillful through practice. Love in any marriage whose romance provides excitement and thrills, is an art. Anyone who becomes an artist at anything does so by developing superior skill in performance. Romance would be constantly in our marriage if more of us were skillful in the fine art of love.

CHAPTER THREE

The Sexual Side of Romance

In Chapter 1 we were reminded that a part of premarital romance depends upon the blocking of sex. We are now concerned with that portion of romance which depends upon the satisfaction of sex in marriage. There is no simple formula. It is not just a matter of anatomy. If it were we could prepare anyone for sex adjustment in marriage in fifteen minutes.

Sex is overwhelmingly psychological and emotional. It involves knowledge and feelings which have been determined and shaped by our experience. Sex is a matter of biology and chemistry, but sex adjustment in marriage is mainly personality adjustment.

Adult Sex Life Is Influenced by Its Background

Our experience with sex depends upon what happened the moment we were conceived, our development through prenatal life, and how we responded to what happened to us after we were born, all through the years until we marry. Our sex life in marriage is, in great measure, predetermined by our sex life before marriage. Since sex is interwoven into personality, this statement cannot be limited to specific acts called sexual.

When parents spank the hand of an infant which has touched its genital organs they are beginning to influence the sex life of their child in its marriage later in life. Assuming that the endocrine glands, of which the sex glands are a part, function normally, the policy used by parents in determining the sex education of their children will greatly influence the experience of those children with sex all through their lives.

If parents punish the child when he asks where he came from, or any other question having to do with sex, the child is taught not to ask parents about such matters. The child also wonders what was so important about that question to cause such an unhappy response from father or mother, and his curiosity is inflated. If curiosity is blocked enough he can become morbid. The only source left for answers is outside the home. Through unintended mishandling many parents force their children to sources that are full of misinformation and surrounded by an atmosphere which may be conducive to mental ill health. Many a married person fails miserably, or is tied up in knots emotionally, in attempting to achieve sex adjustments in marriage because of the treatment of sex in his life as a child by parents who were themselves forced to treat it the way they did—as a result of the way *their* parents handled the matter when they were children.

Some parents answer questions about where babies come from with "little white lies" which include every imaginable evasion. Some "pass the buck" from themselves to the other parent depending on whether it is a boy or a girl who asks and on the assumption that fathers should answer boys and mothers, girls. Perhaps when puberty arrives and there is a natural identification of sons with fathers and mothers with daughters because of like experiences, such a pairing of questions and answers may develop. Before that, either parent could equally well reply. The one presented with the question is the one who should answer.

Perhaps the most awesome policy used by parents is that of saturating sex with sacred sentimentalism to a point where it is nothing but a heavenly fairy tale, or at least so holy as to be untouchable and certainly undiscussable. The next most awesome and perhaps much more damaging relating of religion to sex is in the teaching that sex and sin are synonymous. Sex is neither sacred nor damning. It is just what we make it by our attitudes toward it and our use of it. If we treated the matter of eating as we do sexual matters we would be as ignorant and as confused, as self-conscious and emotionally wrought up about eating as we are about sex.

There is nothing about eating which determines that we shall have a good diet. We could poison our-

selves, starve, or die of gluttony if we lacked sufficient knowledge and control. There is nothing about
a knife which determines how it shall be used: we
may peel potatoes, or we may stab somebody with it.
There is nothing about an automobile which decides
whether it shall be used as a rolling room with picture windows added to our home, or a house of pros-
titution on wheels. Our knowledge of its potentialities and our use of it according to our sense of values
determines the results. The same principles apply to
sex all through life.

Not long ago, and in some minds today, the mention of sex created a mental and an emotional condition best described as panic. Man's earliest experiences with fire had the same effect. Our experience
with sex and fire have been so similar that we have
interchanged the words with which we speak of each
element. When somebody has been hurt by misuse
of sex we say, "They got their fingers burned." We
speak of the person who is unusually stimulating or
who is easily excited sexually as a "hot number." We
talk of the warmth of friendship, the light of inspira-
tion, and the power of achievement and these phrases
may refer to fire or sex. Like fire, sex—when it is out
of control—can burn with consuming passion and
leave only smoking embers amid destruction. So long
as we are careful to learn what fire is, what it can do,
and how to control it and use it constructively we
may have its benefits. We would wreck modern civilization if we were to eliminate fire. We are careful to

teach about it in order that we may deal with it safely.

It would be interesting to see what would happen if we were suddenly to take an attitude toward fire similar to the attitude we have taken toward sex. How safe would our children be if we handled any question they asked about fire by punishing them, or telling white lies, or drawing up beautiful senti- mentalities, or saying, "When you are old enough I will tell you." Some people can answer questions about fire *or* sex without getting hysterical, or feel- ing guilty or somehow dipped in sin. Some people can tell the truth in simple words that are actual words and not silly substitutes. We do not have to give detailed descriptions of the chemical processes involved when we strike a match, nor do we need to scare the daylights out of children with lurid descrip- tions colored by the sort of emotions we might have if caught in a hotel fire, in order to contribute sen- sibly to the education of our children with respect to fire. We do the best job when we know what we are talking about and when our emotions are under control.

A young mother looked out the kitchen window while she was washing dishes one morning and saw her three-year-old daughter being undressed in the middle of the front lawn by the four-year-old boy next door. She uttered a startled cry, grabbed an apron from the closet without drying her hands, and rushed hysterically to the rescue of her daughter.

She hastily wrapped the little girl in the apron, gathered her into her arms, exploded in the little boy's face, and punished her child when she returned to the house. She was under the illusion that she was protecting her child. She had no idea of the damage she may have done to her child and the little boy by her misguided action.

Here was a case where a mother read adult interpretation into childhood action, projected her own feelings into the situation, and rushed to protect. Instead of protection she may have supplied injury with lifelong scars. If she had opened the window and suggested calmly but firmly to her little girl that people do not run around outside without clothes, and that she must get them on or come in, the incident would have passed with much less harm. She might have gone next door and called the little boy's mother's attention to the scene and inquired if her son was that badly in need of satisfying his normal curiosity. In either event both children might have been safeguarded. As it was, both were exposed to a possibly traumatic experience. Some husband twenty years later may wonder why his wife is not able to respond with abandon to his love expressed in the sexual embrace.

Three neighbor women were expressing their reactions to the births of their children. They were sewing together on a quilt as they talked. The daughter of one was playing in an adjoining room. Since there is a certain amount of status to be gained if

James E. Clark

the matter of birth is difficult, and since the first one to tell her experience never has a chance, the review became more and more terrible as each took her turn. By the time all children in each family had been accounted for, the little girl was terrified. The mother did not know that the child had overheard and wondered a few years later, about the girl's abnormal fright when menstruation began. She worried when her daughter seemed uninterested in boys in school, and talked at length with her husband later about her daughter's avoidance of men when she became old enough to marry.

There Is a Price on Ignorance

A woman who had been raised in ignorance (her parents called it innocence) married a man who had learned all he knew about sex from places and persons outside his home—none of which sources was trustworthy—and from his experiences with prostitutes. He wrecked his marriage as far as sex was concerned by attempting to treat his wife according to what he had learned from such an educational background. They had three children but very meager and unsatisfying sex life. The animal act of intercourse was considered sex life. The mother tried to "do her duty" as a wife and submitted to his advances for a while, but the whole matter became more and more resistible. Nature finally responded by revolting, and the wife expressed her rejection through illness.

It was impossible to protect her children from the emotional reactions of her experience with sex in her marriage. She certainly did not make any deliberate attempt to ruin their chances for a successful marriage but she could not refrain from comments such as "All men are beasts," or "Sex is a degrading experience," when any reference to sex was made by her children. Some beautiful, warm, loving wife with normal capacities for the expression of her love through her sexual experiences with her husband may now be wondering why her husband is so uninterested for such long times, or so vicious during those times when he is interested, or so guilt-stricken afterward.

A man who prided himself on being modern fell for the age-old illusion that masculine virility is demonstrated by the sexual exploitation of women. He became quite promiscuous during adolescence, confining himself, however, to the girl he married during the last of their courtship. In spite of his promises made during their wedding, the husband found it all but impossible to confine his sexual experiences to his marriage and threatened it with one escapade of infidelity after another. He and his wife sought counsel from a doctor who was unusual in that he understood the psychological and emotional factors involved. Yet in spite of adequate counsel many months passed before even a relative sense of security was achieved.

Many people seem to think that entering marriage

is like going from one room into another and clos-
ing the door. Well-meaning parents have suggested
to their young people that they "sow their wild oats
and then settle down." Wise ones among the ancients
were smart enough to see through that one. They
observed from human experience that you reap
what you sow. Such advice would suggest that there
is no connection between the sowing and the reap-
ing. It is evidence of our ignorance that some of us
believe that what happens before a wedding has nothing to do with what happens after it. Actually entering marriage is more like going from one room into
another and removing the wall. Whatever is in our
experience before the wedding bells ring will have
much to do with whether our marriage will be full
of the music of chimes, or whether we shall be among
those for whom the bells toll. We take our knowledge and ignorance, our healthy and unhealthy attitudes and feelings, the cumulative effects of all our
acts according to our good, bad, or indifferent philosophy of life right into marriage with us. We are
a good marriage risk or a poor one, to ourselves and
our husband or wife, according to how all these past
experiences, attitudes, and philosophies add up.

Much of the past may be less threatening if what
we need is more adequate knowledge about sex and
we get it. If we understand that attitudes and feelings, recognized as unhealthy and dangerous to good
adjustment, may be reconditioned and if we set
about such reconditioning, more romance may re-

sult. If consultation with some doctor who is trained to understand more than the physical aspects of sex, or with some marriage counselor who is recognized as competent seems indicated and is sought, happiness may be increased.

If we have a satisfying sex life in marriage but do not think we know all there is to know, and do not feel we have developed all the skills there are in the expression of love through sex in marriage, we may achieve even more satisfaction and wonder-filled experience by our continuing to learn. Sex life in marriage is not automatic any more than it is only animal. It is an experimental, explorative adventure which two persons may undertake together over a long period of time. There are degrees of achievement in sex adjustment just as there are in all other aspects of marriage.

Recent surveys have uncovered many facts about sex life in parts of our country and among some of our people. For the most part these surveys reveal the consequences of the ignorance and emotional distortion resulting from the recent period of puritanical prudery which superimposed a conspiracy of silence on everything pertaining to sex. Some people may make the mistake of assuming that these findings represent a desirable pattern of behavior with respect to sex. We have much to learn, and facts from every honest attempt to discover may help to develop a more comprehensive understanding upon which to base our achievement. But no single bit of research can be regarded as a safe guide until it has been related to findings from studies in other areas of human experience which are also involved.

"Doing What Comes Naturally" Is a Romantic Illusion

In both love and sex many people attempt to follow the idea that romance is to be found by doing what comes naturally. Apparently they think that heaven can be achieved here on earth by removing all restrictions and restraints. Those who have tried it seem to run into a little hell instead. Ignorance is bliss until the consequences come along. As a philosophy of life, the idea that we can or should do what comes naturally would be rejected by any thoughtful person.

A person who decided to do what comes naturally about eating would not look for food at a grocery store or meat market. He would run it down and kill it, tear it apart, and eat it while it was still quivering. He would tear out the biggest piece, unless he were a she-with-young. He would go off and squat somewhere and rip into it. If anybody came along he would make noises meaning "Scram," unless the intruder were bigger—in which case he himself would run away. When he finished satisfying his hunger he would drop the remains wherever he was, wipe his mouth on his arm and start looking for water. Napkins, even cloth sleeves, are not natural. Cooking, cutlery, silver, chairs, china, linen, sharing, manners

—all these are the products of not doing what comes naturally.

Not finding any refrigerated fountain or water faucet he would have to hunt for a puddle, or lake, or river to get a drink. He would lean over the edge after making sure that there were no other animals bigger than himself who were also ready to do what came naturally; he would part his hair with his hands or flip it back over his shoulder or just let it soak while he drank. Haircuts are not an evidence of doing what comes naturally. Then he would drink and become a living aquarium, since boiling water or treating it chemicaly to kill germs is not doing what comes naturally. If he slipped in, he would get a bath; otherwise he would not bathe unless he lived in the tropics, in which case he would bathe to keep cool, not to get clean. Bathing for hygienic purposes is not doing what comes naturally.

In no part of our life can we do what comes naturally and have the benefits of culture and civilization at the same time. Nature is restricted and restrained, controlled and directed in order that we may become social beings and develop personalities. Freedom and security—so long as we are members of any group— depend upon this restriction and control. To believe that love and sex are exceptions and that no restriction and restraint, no control and direction are needed is to reveal our ignorance and add to our misery if we act upon it. Such belief leads to action which proves the truth of that old adage, "Most of our miseries are the result of mistaken attempts to secure happiness."

Romance Is Not Found with Sex in the Gutter

Given a man and a woman who have grown up enough for marriage, who have adequate knowledge and healthy attitudes and feelings about sex, who love each other with a mature love—and here are the makings of a real sexual support for romance in marriage. Under such circumstances mutual anticipation might precede sexual intercourse by several hours and make its contribution to the gradual build-up of sex excitement. A prolonged period of "petting" can contribute toward arousal with many shades of psychological and physical sensation. It is conceivable that the experience might take place in light instead of darkness since nothing is wrong and there would be no feeling of shame or need to hide.

Whenever we want to have an unusually enjoyable evening we are concerned with atmosphere. We turn lights low or use candles for a touch of romance. We may secure flowers and arrange them artistically. In some instances we burn incense. We may select music appropriate to the occasion, according to the mood we desire. We do everything we can think of to make the evening one of beauty with the loveliness of surroundings most conducive to it. We would be more courteous and considerate than usual, and do what we could to see that the other had the most enjoyable time possible. But this is a far cry from the sort of surroundings and atmosphere in which sexual intercourse occurs in most marriages. Of course making the effort toward loveliness of surroundings would not be doing what comes naturally, however; so long as we blunder along on an animal level we should not expect more than animal returns.

Why should we use every resource to make life beautiful and meaningful except when sex is involved? Or should we permit such atmosphere and surroundings to contribute only to illicit sex experience? Should not love have such accompaniments? It is true that such surroundings are not the most important aspect of the abundant sex life, but the ability to appreciate their relationship to sex experience may make sex life more meaningful and abundant. For some people, unfortunately, the introduction of sex into such surroundings would ruin the atmosphere. (In such case a little divine fumigation of sex may be indicated!)

We do not invite people who are inconsiderate, or abusive, or just plain rude to any important and enjoyable evening affair. If they become so during the evening we may tolerate them for the rest of the time, but we do not invite them again. On the other hand, how long could we keep a friend if we insisted that he do what he seriously thought he should not do? The best kind of sexual experience in marriage is possible when a husband and a wife are friends. If, in addition, they love each other, and have any skill in expressing that love, one will not be inconsiderate and abusive, and insist that the other do what he seriously does not want to do. Sex life in marriage is not made successful through exploitation, but through loving co-operation.

Talking about their experiences together, revealing to each other what excites and what repels, reexamining the soundness of feelings and the validity of preconceptions with mutual respect and consideration will open up new vistas of romance in marriage as far as sex experience contributes to it. Sex adjustment is never completed. It is a lifelong process of new adventure. The vigor, partial knowledge, and fears of youth are replaced by the satisfactions and appreciations and the self-confidence of age. As personality and environment change, sex expression of love changes, yet here again we tend to measure all of life by some small fragment of it. As with love some people proceed under the illusion that sexual experience at one stage of life should be just as it was at some earlier stage. Romance is in those marriages in which people develop mutually satisfying relationships for every stage of the maturation process.

Better Sex Adjustment Can Be Developed

Moral standards appropriate to life before marriage are not applicable to sex in marriage. That is generally true. Of course such moral standards as honesty and respect for integrity apply all the way through life. The problem arises, however, from failure to realize that a woman cannot develop habits of thinking and feeling about sex under restriction and then, with the pronouncement of a wedding ceremony, suddenly possess the thoughts and feelings that will enable her to respond with passionate abandon. Both husband and wife need to know about how to recondition themselves to have the best chance of bringing about the awakening of sex in the woman's life. Many wives have become mothers several times and experienced no awakening of sex life.

The arousal time in men is much less than in women. For this reason about one-third of all married women never experience orgasm through sexual intercourse with their husbands. The man has completed his experience before the woman has had time to become more than partially aroused. Repeated partial arousal with no satisfaction leaves a woman in a pitch of nervous excitement which may ultimately build resistance and finally rejection. Some men who have "been around" and think they know all the answers do not know this simple fact, or what to do about it. They may conclude that their wives do not love them although their wives may have been submitting for months or years because they love their husbands. A man can conclude that an unresponsive wife is frigid, with no understanding of his own part in bringing frigidity about. When both husband and wife know about this sexual difference between the male and the female, and work together to effect adjustment, sex in their marriage is much more satisfying. Controlling the rate of arousal while stimulating that of his wife is the man's problem. Books and pamphlets dealing with these and other problems are listed in the back of this book under readings appropriate to this chapter.

For many husbands and wives there is only one "right" position for intercourse. Any other position is "improper," "morally tainted," if not actually abnormal, they think. Such feelings represent a part of the distortion resulting from ignorance and the extremes of puritanical prudishness mentioned before. Any position which does not injure physically or psychologically is as moral as any other position. The idea that intercourse should stop when pregnancy is discovered is obsolete. The doctor providing prenatal care may indicate that it may continue up to the fifth, sixth, or seventh month according to his judgment of the progress of the pregnancy. He may advise various positions as a matter of good sense and in the interests of the best health for all concerned.

What Is Normal and What Is Abnormal?

There is considerable confusion about what is normal and what is abnormal regarding sex, in and out of marriage. Not long ago we attempted to scare children and adolescents into "being good" by telling them all sorts of fearful things about the consequences of masturbation. The practice of self-stimulation is practically unknown among societies which permit mating upon the arrival of puberty. In our country we have good reason to restrict mating to marriage, and we feel that people should not marry until they are ready to assume the responsibilities involved.

Marriage here is pushed some years beyond puberty, and masturbation develops as a substitute for mating. Unless the practice becomes so firmly established that it competes with intercourse in marriage there is little harm in it. If guilt feelings are developed, there may be considerable harm in the guilt feelings. Such feelings have been induced frequently by well-meaning parents. They can become so severe that they make it impossible for a person to be successful at anything. In rare cases they have induced feelings of eternal damnation and resulted in attempts at suicide. When a married couple engage in sexual intercourse, masturbation—mutual or otherwise—may be a normal part of the arousal process.

When two persons of the same sex engage in mutual sexual stimulation we call it homosexuality. Yet it is quite possible for two persons of the same sex to have a homosexual relationship with no expression of a sex act whatever. The word "homosexual" has been loaded with so much fear and panic and vicious public condemnation that we cannot even think about it intelligently. The word homosexual means "of the same sex." When we speak of women in general we are speaking of a homosexual segment of the human race. Any organization which has only men in it is a homosexual organization since it is made up of members of only one sex. But the word is dynamite. Ignorance, emotional distortion, and no little amount of guilt and self-righteousness have combined to cause us to use it only when we intend it to mean the arousal of sexual excitement between two persons of the same sex. A large percentage of our population experience such desire at some time during their life and, as in the case of love, feeling the desire is not the important thing. What one does about it is important.

Nobody is altogether, absolutely and exclusively, either male or female. Everybody has something of both sexes in his physiological and psychological make-up. In some respects a few men are more feminine than the average woman. Some women are more masculine than the average man. Our limited knowledge of sex causes a large majority of us to assume that sex is determined by whether we have male or female genital organs. In our ignorance we think that size of these organs has something to do with the extremes of maleness or femaleness. We are a pretty well-mixed-up people, with some showing signs of extremes in maleness and femaleness, but the majority ranging somewhere in between with signs of both apparent. Everybody is more one sex than the other, with the exception of a small minority who become medical and psychological problems. But in spite of all the variety, all the variations of sexuality, society approves only the heterosexual relationship, which is the relationship between the male and the female.

There is good reason for our approval, but there is no good reason for the unintelligent and cruel way in which we handle those who arouse our disapproval.

Our personal and social attitudes toward people who have been accused of homosexuality and other abnormalities is similar to the attitudes we used to take toward the mentally ill. It may be for the same reason: we did not understand the mentally ill, therefore we imprisoned them and flogged the more violent ones or chained them in the dungeon. When we gained sufficient knowledge to understand them we began to treat them differently. Perhaps better understanding is what is needed with regard to sex and those who seem to us abnormal. Mental illness may be either a cause or an effect of sexual abnormality; or the abnormality may be just this person's way of adjusting to life because of biological development, or the influence of parents through childhood, or other conditioning experiences across the years. Sexual abnormality may be caused by factors which have no direct connection with sex whatsoever. We have a lot to learn, and our intolerance proves it.

Abnormalities Have Natural Causes

If you block a stream you must provide a controlled outlet, or the stream will find its own outlets. These uncontrolled outlets may destroy the dam, or cause a lot of damage around and below it. If we block sex from its normal expression in mating at the arrival of puberty, for the purpose of gaining some values otherwise impossible, we must provide controlled outlets supported by intelligent social approval. Sex cannot be safely repressed any more than it would be safe to build a dam and never let any water by; or to tie the lid down on a tea kettle, put a stopper in the spout, and keep the fire burning under it. As far as sex is concerned in our lives the river will continue to flow; the fire will continue to burn. There is no way of drying up the springs or turning out the fire. We must find sensible, socially approved outlets for sex before marriage or we will get "abnormalities." There need be no such problem in marriage unless it is brought into marriage from habits established before marriage. Sometimes the normal experience of sex adjustment in marriage solves the problem and the so-called abnormality disappears. If it does not disappear, professional consultation is indicated.

Not all behavior called abnormal is abnormal, or unnatural, or a violation of "the highest and best" we know. We might profit by a re-examination of our concepts of what abnormality is. Sometimes our frightened or hysterically prejudiced attitude, devoid of any real intelligence, is more abnormal than the sexual deviation which causes us to be so unrighteously righteous. Our general public attitude toward persons accused of sexual abnormality, when we get excited, is very close to mass mental illness. God knows that some terrible things happen, but we do not help ourselves or anybody else by getting into a terrible state of mental and emotional incompetence as a result.

We have made advances. Today no one need feel the terror formerly associated with discovery of "skeletons in the closet" when someone on the family tree is mentally ill. Most of us are "not quite right in our minds" a good portion of the time, and present estimates suggest that one out of every eight of us will need hospitalization for mental illness some time or other before we die. We shall not receive it because there are not that many hospital beds in the country. But certainly we no longer chain the mentally ill in prisons and whip them when they become violent because they are not able to control themselves. Such attitude and treatment today would be considered abnormal. There will come a time when many of our present attitudes and actions with respect to "sex offenders" will be considered abnormal, and we shall realize that we may be able to head off some "terrible maniac" before the danger stage is reached.

If we are to be successful in our marriage, men will need to understand the sex life of the male. Married men would do well to check up on what they know, to see which part may be valid and which part error. Women need to know more about the sex life of the female, and which part of their preconceived ideas and beliefs are sound, and which part utterly untrue. Both men and women need to understand the sex life of the other far more comprehensively than most married people do. Such knowledge will include anatomy and the process of reproduction, but it will also include the psychological, social, philosophical, and spiritual aspects of sex life. It will have to include some knowledge of the relation of all this to our culture, in order that sex morality may be modified where it needs to be, and supported where our freedom and security are at stake. Such education should begin with great-grandparents, ideally, but certainly with the little child, and continue through all the years of its growing up according to its needs.

We do not have all the knowledge about sex which we need, but we do have more than we have had. Good books are now available which may help any couple to more successful experience. It is a wise husband and wife who deliberately search for more insight and understanding in order to improve this part of their marriage relationship. It is a happy husband and wife who succeed in discovering the satisfactions possible through such understanding and patient achievement through the years. Romance becomes distinctly their own through successful sex adjustment, more than through any other experience in their marriage.

CHAPTER FOUR

The Relation of Romance to Relations with Relatives

Those of us who have been married long have discovered that relatives can have a lot to do with our romance. We have found out the real truth about the romantic assertion that marriage is a private affair. Since no two persons live alone on some other planet and since all of us come from some family, relatives are inevitable. From one point of view we contribute them to each other. From another point of view we married them when we married our husband or wife. The ardent lover who avowed with heat, "I am marrying *you*. I am *not* marrying your family!" undoubtedly meant it for a convincing pronouncement of adoration. But he has long since found out that he was only revealing his ignorance. The discovery of his error may have been painful and may have caused him to add his part to the litter of in-law complaints and bitterness thinly coated with alleged humor. Or, he may have discovered to his delight that he is indeed a fortunate man to have such likable kinsfolk.

In time, the sweet young wife who, crossed-up with her husband's parents, suggests a move to Alaska, may discover that distance does not solve all problems arising from conflict with relatives. The direct contacts and open conflicts may be eliminated, but we take our families along with us wherever we go, in our attitudes toward life, in what we think makes a home, what we expect of each other and the sort of people we have become. Relatives are not easily eliminated. We have them supporting our romance, or threatening it. If we do not have good relationships we have in-law troubles running all the way from the slightly irritating to the desperately unbearable.

Relatives Matter

In a marriage where in-law relationships are fine, romance may be stronger and more colorful. Bob and Marge knew it well. They loved their own parents and the parents they acquired through their marriage. Parents on both sides enjoyed being in their home and were glad to have them visit in theirs. Nobody seemed to be trying to run anybody's life for them, and nobody was always telling others how to run their marriage. They did not always agree on everything, but they had learned how to agree to disagree without loss of respect and affection. Everybody had grown up to an adult level and they treated each other accordingly. Parents had stopped being parents and the young married people had stopped being children.

The fact that everybody was related did not cancel individual rights and responsibilities of persons to persons. There were happy notes of surprise and genuine expressions of pleasure when in-laws dropped in. Out of simple regard for courtesy and convenience, nobody overstayed a welcome. They kept in touch because everybody really liked everybody, were interested in what happened, and were always ready to encourage or help. There was a pride in their relationships which was audible in any reference one made to the others. It was rare, but it was wonderful, and Bob and Marge knew how it added to the thrills and adventure of their romance.

George and Roberta were not so fortunate. Romance was seriously threatened in their marriage. To illustrate, once when they wanted to go on a vacation George's parents thought that it would cost too much and insisted that the money needed for it would be better spent in furnishing their house. Everybody argued about it. George's parents were looking at things from their point of view and still acting like parents. George and Roberta did not care so much about the furniture or the vacation as they did about freedom to run their own affairs. The real issue was not whether a vacation was wise, but whether George's parents could still make decisions for him.

The more they argued the more unhappy everybody became. Roberta finally asked George if he was always going to let his parents make up his mind for him, and he exploded. Some of his pent-up emotional resistance to his parents was directed toward his wife. When Roberta's parents heard about it they encouraged the young couple to go on the vacation and volunteered to supply some of the expense money if needed. That put George in the position of secretly wishing that his parents were more like Roberta's, and then he felt guilty because he really loved his parents. He defended them too much, accused Roberta of feeling superior, became angry in the conflict which followed, and began to hate his own parents. When George's parents discovered the attitude of Roberta's parents they became furious, and everybody was miserable. George's parents simply could not stop being parents, and because their parenthood had lingered too long, George was not quite grown up. The relationship was one of dominance and submission, at best interference, and the community saw it as in-law troubles. Romance was smothered under gloom.

Parents Must Graduate, Too

The main job of parents is to make themselves useless as parents. That is done according to their skill in helping their children grow toward responsible independence. It takes responsible independence to make marriage work and produce romance. Here is one of the more important reasons why there are varying degrees of success in marriage, and considerable differences in the amount and quality of romance in marriage. There seem to be varying degrees of independence and dependence, of responsibility and irresponsibility, characteristic of people who marry.

Some married people had to secure their independence from parents by revolt. They had to pay so much attention to revolting that they never did develop enough responsibility to go with the independence they sought. They may have secured their independence, but they are a threat to themselves and others for lack of enough responsibility.

Some are still revolting in the marriage, having transferred their antagonism from mother to wife, or father to husband. They married before they were grown up enough for marriage. Their only hope is for them to grow up in their marriage. In this instance it would mean the development of sufficient responsibility to change threat into support.

Some parents have not grown up sufficiently as persons. They cannot contribute toward the responsible independence of their children beyond their own immaturity. Such parents are likely to feel that their children cannot rely on themselves and therefore continue to insist that their grown children rely on them. They do not seem to realize that continued insistence upon making decisions for their children after they have reached adulthood is confession of the failure of their parenthood. Unless young adults from such homes can understand that the problem is one of immaturity, and find out what they can do to contribute toward their own maturity, the vicious cycle may go on from generation to generation.

A young married person upon discovering that his parent is immature usually wants to change the parent toward maturity. But young people who have reached adulthood have no more right to try to live their parents' lives for them than their parents have a right to live the lives of their young adults for them. The best method of adjusting to immature parents is to understand what is to be expected and to expect it. We are irritated when we expect anything else. Knowing what to expect we are ready for it or can adjust to it much more quickly and easily than if we did not know or were unwilling to accept our parents as they are. But being able to do that depends upon whether we grow up. Immature young adults, married or single, cannot accept immature parents any more than their parents can accept them. The struggle to let people be themselves and adjust to that circumstance is a part of the maturation process.

All of us who have parents or who are parents should realize that parenthood is a function which should have an end. If the purpose of parenthood has not been completed it cannot end. If parenthood is not terminated everybody involved will be handicapped accordingly in their attempts to deal with the requirements of adult life. All relationships may be affected, but those relationships in marriage, and with in-laws, will be particularly threatened. Romance will be sickly, if it remains alive.

It is not easy for parents to stop being parents. They have been doing it for a long time by the time their child reaches adulthood, and it is difficult to bring parenthood to an end. Habits of thinking and feeling are well established and may have to be broken, or may be too strong to break. They should have been modified constantly throughout the years of childhood and youth of their children. Even that is not possible without some struggle and pain.

Parents start out with a child completely dependent upon its mother. Nature moves the new life toward independence through growth and development across the nine months of pregnancy. Her purpose is to produce a baby capable of surviving with less dependence when it is born. Even then it needs parental care and protection in almost every way except its own bodily processes of breathing, digesting, eliminating, and growing. It is very satisfying to most parents to be needed so completely. It is irritating to some parents to have to take care of children because they interfere with the sort of "freedom" that characterizes irresponsible independence.

Parents have responsibility to do whatever is needed for their children until their children can do for themselves. Adequate parenthood is constantly striving to help children to do for themselves. Parenthood should be withdrawn at whatever rate children demonstrate that they can do for themselves.

But that means that parents are needed less and less and finally not at all. The threat to most of us parents is that we need to be needed. That need is so great in some of us that it slows down parenthood until it lags behind the age of the child and trouble is sure to follow. It is when children become young people ahead of adequate parenthood for youth, or young people marry when parenthood is back in the teens somewhere that trouble with in-laws is likely to develop. When parenthood lags, childhood and youth are prolonged if not stopped somewhere along the process of growth. If children have not grown up by the time they have become adults and married, their immaturity can complicate in-law relationships and threaten romance.

It is hard for some parents to realize that their children have grown up even when there is no question about it in the minds of others. They have known their children so long as children that it is hard for them to think of their young adults as anything but big children. Some parents seem to watch for signs which prove that their grown young adults are too young to be living their lives by themselves. Any decision except the one the parents would make is frequently interpreted as such proof. Some parents are unwilling to see their children make mistakes, and deny them a valuable learning opportunity. Some cannot stand to see their children experience disappointment and arrange things with the result that their children have little chance to learn to deal with disappointment. Such parents are likely to continue trying to keep their children from making mistakes or being disappointed when they are old enough to marry, and on into their marriage. Frequently young adults have to resist such parental interference or remain dependent, or gain their freedom at the price of affections. Some parents viciously misuse love as a weapon with which to maintain their dominance. If their young adult breaks free in order to assume responsibility denied by his parent, that is taken to mean that he no longer loves his parent. So thoroughly do some parents succeed in teaching their children that any action otherwise than the parents want it is proof of disloyalty and disrespect, that some parents are more of a threat to their grown children after the parents die than they were while they remained alive. It is easier to rebel against living parents than to violate their memory after they have passed away.

Some married people are fortunate in having had parents who, wisely, had developed the skills needed to provide increasing freedom for their children while they were growing toward adulthood. Children with such parents learn to develop their own abilities and to assume responsibilities which go with such independence. Parents of such children did not let them make fatal mistakes, but they did not consider that all mistakes are fatal. They provided opportunities for their children to practice making decisions, encouraged them even when they made a wrong one, and let their children know that they were loved no matter what happened. Perhaps the most important thing about their parenthood was that they did not expect too much.

When parenthood has been unfortunate or unwise in the eyes of young adults there is a natural tendency for them to go in the opposite direction when they become parents. Or they may repeat the mistake their parents made, but go to even greater extremes with their children. In any instance where married people may have cause to feel that their parents made a mistake with them, the wisest thing is to make a serious study of parenthood under the guidance of some competent person or agency. As the past is more thoroughly understood, feelings about it may change, and policies may be established which result in a much healthier parenthood. Such a study would include an effort to see how childhood experiences affect marriage relationships. One's own marriage may be improved with a consequent increase of romance.

In-Laws Are Outsiders

When any young man approaches marriage with any young woman he is in competition with her father. Neither he nor her father may intend it, but she has been a little girl for a long time and her father has been the one man in her life from whom she learned about men. That could not happen without heartstrings getting all tangled up together. Even the mature father feels some sharp thrust of jealousy at the thought of another man in his daughter's life. If the father is immature he will resent this intrusion, probably criticize enough to make his daughter unhappy, force defense and rebellion upon her, and generally move things toward unhappy-in-law relationships if she marries. Such a father might object to any man in whom his daughter showed unusual interest. He might compete for his daughter's love and regard even after she was married. Too many women have been made the battleground upon which a husband and father fight for the young woman's favor. Romance is usually severely wounded in the fight. When a woman is aware of what is happening and its possible significance in her life she may be able to help each of her men toward better relationships. She may have to have the help of some trusted friend or counselor, but everybody will stand to gain and romance may acquire new vitality.

Daughters and wives, however, are not always innocent parties to this struggle. It is not unheard of for a woman to attempt to play one man against the other and get all she can out of each. If she does she is not ready for marriage, whether she is already married or not; and she follows this policy at the risk of losing romance, if not her marriage as well.

When a father is competing, and the young husband can understand, even if the father cannot, then the young husband may do much to help develop better relationships. But some husbands do not understand and are very jealous of their wife's father, thus making things miserable for everybody. This is particularly likely if the husband had to rebel from his own parents' domination. He transfers his thinking and feeling toward his own parents to his wife's parents, and does all he can to win her away from them completely.

There is a somewhat similar situation when any young woman approaches marriage with any mother's son. Every normal mother feels a touch of jealousy. The mature mother controls it. The immature mother cannot. Any other woman is an invader. Some mothers are considerably disturbed over their own conflict created by the need for their son and by the knowledge that their son should have a wife. Some women feel guilty for resenting their son's wife and lean over backward in efforts to be nice to the daughter-in-law. Some daughters-in-law have similar feelings and overdo in their efforts to be nice, too. It does not always work, for women seem to have a knack of knowing, perhaps even better than men, when they are being insincere with each other.

The mother who understands her own feelings and can control them may contribute much to the romance of her son's marriage. The son who understands the rivalry between his wife and his mother may do much to tone it down or eliminate it. The maturity of all involved will decide the outcome. The wife who understands this struggle in her mother-in-law may do much to help establish the best of relationships. One who does not understand, or who is incapable because of immaturity, will probably do all that she can to wean her husband from any relationship with his family, and his mother will be considered her chief threat. Many a man has become a bone of contention between his mother and his wife, both of whom use all their feminine wiles in efforts to win him.

When a husband or a wife feels that the only safety in the marriage is to be achieved by winning the other from his parents and family completely, there is strong likelihood that love life and general growth of personality was slowed down or arrested on a level too immature for marriage to be successful enough for multicolored romance. On the other hand, it could mean that parenthood was arrested in its development and that "child fixation" is causing parents to interfere with the young marriage. In either instance blame and condemnation from any angle will do little but make matters worse. Efforts at sympathetic understanding and patience are more likely to help. Counsel from a trained marriage counselor, or a serious attempt to better the situation through consultation with a competent psychiatrist, might bring romance out of the thunder clouds of threatening in-law immaturities.

A person who is insecure for lack of self-confidence may be afraid that his in-laws will not like him. This fear may persist on into marriage. If it does he will watch for signs that his in-laws do not approve of him. Because he is watching for such signs he may interpret almost any word or act of in-laws as proof that they do not like him. If he reaches that conclusion he may begin to act as if his in-laws were hostile to him, and thereby cause them not to like him. This vicious circle of fear is self-destructive and is painful proof that fear can create the very thing feared, at least in relations with relatives. Romance cannot survive in an atmosphere of fear, especially fear of one's own inadequacy.

In-Laws Are People, Too

It would seem to be easy for relatives to take things for granted with each other. The risk is that they may take so much for granted that they leave out such important little things as thoughtfulness and simple courtesy. One need only remember that relatives are people, too, with all the sensitiveness and desires to be respected and regarded highly that any person might have. Much in-law trouble could be avoided if relatives acted toward each other as if they were not relatives. Some of us want our relatives to feel freer with us, but we do not want that desire to be interpreted as freedom to take advantage. Some relatives enjoy dropping in unannounced and some of us like it. Others prefer to have time to clean up a bit and would rather have notice of our coming. Relatives who know each other well usually adjust to individual differences.

Tim had two brothers and a sister, all married. He

and his wife enjoyed visiting them. Tim knew that Ray and his wife would not care in what condition they found them, or their house, and would gladly welcome them with genuine pleasure no matter whether they arrived during the day or any hour of the night, with or without notice. Bruce and his wife would be just as glad to see them but they would not be so loud about it, and they preferred to know, at least a few hours before they arrived, that company was coming. Bea and her husband reacted according to mood, therefore Tim played it safe and always let them know. With Ray and family there was never any tension over anything. Everybody was relaxed and had fun. At Bruce's home it was a matter of being on guard and careful, or someone might be offended when no offence was intended. They had fun, but it was a strained sort of fun. All persons were more relaxed after they separated. Understanding his relatives, Tim and his wife were able by adaptability to enjoy their fellowship and companionship, and make their visits enjoyable to their relatives.

One reason for strained relationships among relatives is our tendency to assume that they think and feel as we do. It would not make any difference to us whether they called before they arrived, so we assume that it should make no difference to them, and we do not call. If they show signs of irritation we "bulldoze" over things because "they should not be that way." But all our assuming and bulldozing will not change them. People who push people around do not change them—they only push people around.

If we are easily offended ourselves we may be overly careful in the precise manner in which we prepare relatives for our visit. We may be so very careful while we are there that it makes them uncomfortable. Under such walking-on-eggs conditions somebody can easily decide that an offense has been committed and apologize when there was no offense. The offense may be denied, and a duel of apologies begins. Sooner or later someone may have to apologize for not accepting an apology and when that attempt to win is rebuffed everybody is in a huff. You can't win!

It could be said that when likable people visit likable people the fact that they are relatives may only increase the fair weather relations. When likable people visit unlikable people, relatives or otherwise, it clouds up and gets chilly. But when unlovely people visit unlovely people, especially when all are relatives, it is pretty sure to be stormy.

When two persons marry, a wife may be in love with her husband but her parents are not. A husband may be in love with his wife but his parents are not. In-laws may have attitudes which indicate a willingness to try, but loving an in-law is a developmental matter requiring time and effort. Relationships could be rapidly improved if we would keep in mind that many of the best elements of courtship are usable with relatives and might produce amazingly happy results.

Some parents like a son-in-law or daughter-in-law in the same way they like anything with which their son or daughter is fascinated. They really only tolerate the son-in-law because their own daughter loves him. Such parental attitude is asking for trouble.

A young woman's parents felt that way about her husband. Everything was fine as long as she was happy. When she became peeved or offended, the parents concluded that the son-in-law was undoubtedly to blame and brought pressure on him to apologize and make things right. It did not work. The marriage was wrecked, but long before that, romance was gone.

Some parents come to love a son-in-law or daughter-in-law for the simple reason that he or she is a lovable person, and parents are loving people. It does not usually happen unless and until all parties know each other fairly well. It would be drastic treatment to require all young married couples to spend six months in the home of each set of parents within two years after their wedding. Such an acquaintance period would completely destroy relations with some relatives, but where adjustments could be made it could build priceless relationships full of happy memories. With many people you have only to know them well to love them.

The prophets of gloom all intone the dirge, "No one roof is big enough to cover two families," especially if they are relatives. But it depends upon the families. Many a roof has been big enough to cover more than two in an emergency. It can be done if people are mature and loving and lovable. There is no better way for people to get acquainted than to have to live together for a while. If they are successful in getting acquainted the experience may be full of excitement and adventure. If they are not successful, in-law relationships may be threatening and that part of romance affected by in-law relationships may be destroyed. No one has any in-laws without being an in-law. In-law relationships are pleasant, desirable, and full of excitement and adventure if we who are in-laws are pleasant, desirable, adventuresome, and exciting people. Relations with relatives depend upon the nature of the people in the relationship. So does romance in marriage.

CHAPTER FIVE

The Relation of Money to Romance

Conflict over money ranks high among the top causes of trouble in marriage according to research thus far. The greatest conflict appears in those marriages to be found among the highest-income brackets. Considerable trouble over financial problems shows up in marriages on the lowest-income levels, too. Married people of moderate income apparently have less conflict than those on a high or low level. Research also shows that nobody is satisfied with his income, whatever it is, and everybody seems to think that if he could only make more money all his troubles would be over. Perhaps this idea arises from the fact that most of us want more than we can afford and tend to buy more than we can pay for. It has been suggested that one way to establish your cost of living when making out your income tax report would be to take your income and add to it ten per cent. Undoubtedly there is some conflict in marriage due to overbuying.

A careful study of money troubles in marriage shows many causes. Bad management is chief among them. Traditional attitudes and expectations regarding who should earn and spend money contribute their share. This is particularly true when two persons in a marriage come from family backgrounds where money has been handled quite differently. In addition, what may appear on the surface to be financial trouble, may actually be personality conflict, with the bills at the end of the month merely the battleground. Emotional instability can also express itself financially. Whatever the cause, when money and conflict are tangled up in marriage, romance is seriously threatened.

Who Earns the Money?

For centuries man has been the breadwinner. From the days of the cave man it has been his job to bring home the bacon. If he could feed, clothe, and shelter his family he could feel respectable in his community. He did all the earning and therefore most if not all of the buying. He handled all financial affairs and all went well. Then man discovered how to apply power to machinery and touched off an industrial revolution, which brought about a family revolution—which changed the financial picture in the home.

Industry began to accomplish outside the home much of the work formerly done in the home by women or under their supervision. Employers began to hire women to do much of what they used to do in the home; but now they were paid for it in dollars and cents. This brought about a new freedom for women. Until then they had depended upon their fathers for existence until they married, and then upon their husbands. Money in their own right brought economic independence, and the move toward "equality of the sexes" was on. Today more than half the homes and farms in our country are in the names of women. Women held more than one-fourth of all the jobs in the nation before World War II. According to a recent national survey it is estimated that around 80 per cent of all inheritance comes to women, and about the same percentage of life insurance beneficiaries are women. Conservative estimates suggest that women control about 40 per cent of the entire national income.

Today nearly 50 per cent of all women employed in full- or part-time jobs are married. The man is no longer the sole breadwinner. In many marriages the wife is making as much money as her husband and in some marriages she makes more than her husband. These changes could not occur without forcing changes in husband-wife relationships. Most young married men today are able to adjust to the team contribution to family income, but some are seriously threatened at the point of their ego, or self-regard, if their wife is employed. This threat is possible even when a husband agrees to the plan of a joint income. If his wife makes more than he does, a husband can be made to feel inferior because he may think of himself in the role of former husbands who were the sole providers, and conclude that he is falling down on the job. In many instances the masculine ego is tied up with the role of breadwinning, and if the wife works romance may be dulled. It may be made brighter if he can change his attitude toward her working and toward himself because of it. If he can realize that his feelings are caused by expecting of himself what fitted nicely into his grandfather's day, but what does not necessarily fit into today's world, he may respect himself as much as his grandfather ever did, and realize that he is just as much a man.

When a husband cannot stand the threat to his masculine ego which may result from his wife's being engaged in gainful occupation, and takes an authoritarian attitude of masculine dominance, he may contribute to his own unhappiness in marriage because of the effect upon his wife. There are few women today who can play the role of their great-grandmothers and be happy. Women have moved toward democracy in family relationships and expect that their rights as persons should be regarded and respected.

Some women need to secure a paying job for reassurance of their feelings of worth in our time when nearly all values are declared in terms of money. Some wives recognize that total family income can be increased if they too accept employment. Some just do not like housework and prefer to employ someone else to do it. A wife may feel that she must work, in spite of parental responsibilities, in order that the family may have what it needs. Experience in some job compatible with marriage may prove invaluable if the husband is temporarily or permanently incapacitated, or if his death throws total financial responsibility suddenly upon the wife. There are many reasons why women want to work in gainful occupation today. Some reasons may be justified, others not. But if a husband takes a patriarchal stand with a wife who must live in a democratic home to be happy, he is threatening her emotional health, and asking for resentment toward himself if not hostility, which can develop beneath the surface of love and eat away at the foundations of romance.

In marital conflict over who earns the money, discussion may lead to understanding, and understanding may contribute toward adjustment as surely as with conflict for whatever cause. A wife may need to understand that a husband cannot change overnight even when he thinks he should and tries to do so. Emotional attitudes are not so easily reconditioned as intellectual concepts, especially when they are tied up with the ego. A husband needs to understand that his wife may not fit the traditional picture of "the woman's place is in the home," at least to perfection, and that she may have needs as a person which require consideration if he loves her for herself, and not just as an instrument for his own satisfaction. He might find marriage more successful if he could realize that compromise may not be any easier for his wife than it is for him. A re-examination of expectations on the part of both husband and wife to see if they are traditional only, or if they fit the circumstances of today's world, grounded in practical considerations, may enable a couple to work out financial problems arising in the emotions.

Who Spends the Money?

Great-grandfather, in his role as father, had control of the purse strings and everybody came to him for money. He may have doled it out according to plan and most considerately to everybody, but everybody including his wife had to ask him for it. He made all decisions about how it should be spent. He occupied a throne in an economic autocracy called the patriarchal family, and even if he was a benevolent despot he was a financial dictator. Only a woman who feels inferior and is happy to be subservient can find romance with such a man and contribute toward his romance today.

There are such men and there are such women. If they get together in a marriage everything may work out fine. But our ideas about love cause some men to enter marriage with a woman who cannot be a servant, and the battle is on. More and more women resent the idea of going to their husband for money every time they need it. Most of the family buying is done by women today. There are those who say that most of all the spending is done by women. Some women can get their husbands and their marriage into hot water by unwise spending, but women in general seem to be pretty good at handling money. Increasing numbers of men are recognizing ability in their wives and leaving to them the fine art of juggling the budget. Today, in approximately one-third of all our families in this country women manage all the money, whether they contribute toward the family income or the husband is the sole provider.

In some families the paycheck is split up according to a divided responsibility. In others a joint checking account is used, although now and then some wife is afraid to check on it without her husband's consent. In one family the husband does all the grocery buying for the simple reason that he is a better buyer than his wife. Both recognize it, and decision was reached by considered judgment and agreement. There seems to be no threat to the husband's masculine ego in doing this traditionally woman's job. His wife does not feel inferior because there are other activities involved in family life in which she is superior, and it all balances up. As a result they acquire more for their money.

If both husband and wife are contributing to the family income it may be easy for each to think of his own earnings as his own money and spend accordingly. Some plan will of necessity have to be worked out, but a good way for a wife to add to conflict over finances is to remind her husband that she is spending her own money. They are in a "we" relationship, but each may operate as if it were "my" money. They are married, except financially. Wives have no option on this trouble-making attitude. A husband may try to act about money as if he were single instead of married, or sole owner of the marriage.

Men and women do not always see things alike nor do they value things alike. There have been frequent fireworks in marriage because a wife bought something which she prized highly and her husband could see no value whatever in it. A man can cause volcanic eruptions by purchasing some long-desired "thing," which looks to his wife like an inexcusable waste of money. Projecting our own evaluations upon others, especially in marriage, can cause trouble over finances. Accepting the fact of individual differences and of the right to act accordingly is not easy, but such an attitude contributes toward harmony in marriage and smooth sailing on financial seas.

Beware of Financial Traps

Some married people are in financial trouble for years because they entered marriage with too little money to begin with. The romantic idea that two can live as cheaply as one is true only if one does not eat. What is meant is that two can live together less expensively than two can live separately but, as is always the case with such generalizations, it depends upon the two. More than one couple have fallen in love and landed in marriage only to discover that they were in a monetary trap. Some have survived by facing the situation realistically, battled to make a go of it on a very meager income, and dug their way out by means of both partners' working.

Borrowing money may be a very wise thing to do, but not all loans are secured in wisdom. Two attitudes can prove to be treacherous. The attitude of the person who swears that he will never borrow a cent, declaring that he will follow a pay-as-you-go plan or none at all, can be a cause of hardship which is quite unnecessary. The very opposite attitude where a person borrows and then borrows again to pay for unwise buying may cause a person to come to the end of his credit rope and hang himself in bankruptcy. It is a bitter pill for a married man to have to admit that he cannot handle his financial affairs, but the person who, admitting it, seeks the help of some capable financial adviser, is likely to come out on top much sooner, and with less pain than the person who tries to cover it up.

Charge accounts and other means of installment buying are just other forms of borrowing. Much of this country's business, personal and corporate, is done on credit. Our credit system has permitted us to achieve beyond what is likely under any other system. But installment buying can become a money trap to those who follow impulse and have never learned to control desire. All our psychology of salesmanship is calculated to induce buying, whether we can afford to buy or not. Business and industry have employed some of the best psychologists in the world to persuade the public to buy. Consumers in general are not organized as business is, and none of the world's great psychologists are being paid to help the public develop sales resistance. Business and industry spend thousands yearly in training salesmen in the art of selling. Only recently have small groups, in and out of school, had much chance for training in the art of buying. Purchase by impulse is a threat to the harmony of many a marriage, and it is debatable whether women have much, if any, edge over men in this threat to romance.

The personal immaturity which reveals itself in the compulsive need to "keep up with the Joneses" can lead marriage into the proverbial financial hole. This influence may involve a house, automobile, landscaping, furnishing, clothes, recreational equipment, or almost anything else. The financial struggle here, like many other points of money troubles, is not a matter of dollars and cents, but of personality and philosophy of life. The solution is not in acquiring more money because there are more and better Joneses. This trap can be avoided only through revising one's outlook on life, reorganizing one's sense of values, or just plain growing up. A person may need to discover why it is so important to keep up with the Joneses. That discovery involves self-examination, and almost any good book on the development of personality will help with the understanding that children depend upon others for their self-regard. Those who reach adulthood and still depend upon others for their feelings about themselves have never grown up. Marriage is for people who have matured, if they want romance.

Another trap is disclosed in the assumption that if one can make a lot of money he can also spend it wisely. Many a person is a financial success in making money but a financial failure in spending it. Much of the trouble in the higher-income brackets is due to this fact. The nurture of those abilities which are needed to be successful in one part of our life does not automatically develop all the rest of our abilities needed to deal with the remaining problems of life. We do not have to fall into any of these traps; or at least we do not have to remain in them and be miserable if we have already fallen.

The Monetary Road to Romance
Is a Winding Road

Financial success in marriage and family affairs is a business. If financial aspects of marriage are approached and handled in a truly businesslike manner a couple may have every chance of romance in their marriage as far as money is concerned. But romantic ideas have prevented our approaching marriage with anything like the same preparation we would make to be successful in any other job. That is true as far as planning to make money stretch and keeping records are concerned. Those who find themselves in a marriage without having developed the skills of managing money well would gain much in taking whatever course of training might be indicated if they are to make the financial part of marriage pay off in romance.

In the democratic family all members are included in discussion of financial matters. Parents may reserve some of the more serious problems for private discussion, but the preparation of their children for successful handling of money in their own marriages years later depends greatly upon whether they are given a chance to learn in their childhood homes. Money matters are worked out best when parents consider themselves members of the board of directors and when all "stockholders" have a share in the establishment of policies governing family finance. A look into the financial state of affairs in any home where there are no established policies will reveal their importance immediately. The way out is through discovery of all ways and means of earning, discussion of individual and family needs, and agreements governing spending. These agreements are the policies which determine success or failure in family finance.

Such policies or agreements should include decisions about who shall earn the money and who shall spend it. Lacking such a businesslike approach to marriage, most couples have to take about seven years to achieve adjustments which will reduce conflict over money matters to a point of no great concern. Management is the great problem. For a lack of it many couples are destroying their chances for romance. Where good management exists, there one finds books and records, filing equipment, and whatever else makes for efficient business and people who know how to use these facilities. The future is plotted on the basis of a factual record of the past. Planning is a key to success in marriage as it is in any other business.

Long-term planning enables some married people to appear to have no financial problems. Some marriages are under strain because there was no planning for children even after they were discovered to be on the way. Unforeseen emergencies can throw a marriage off the track unless there is some plan to enable the couple to meet them. Accident, unemployment, illness, depression, financial reverses in business and many other unpredictable crises may threaten unless there has been adequate planning to provide for them. Too many couples are living in resentful misery during the retirement years after children have grown up and gone because there was no planning for the time of less economic productivity.

Many a family could do more of the things they want to do on their present income if their money were managed better. Most of us could have some of the things now beyond our reach if we knew how to make our money go further. Unnecessary conflict exists in some marriages where there is money enough if the couple only knew how to use it. Love may be the most important thing in marriage but it grows strongest when it rests on a balanced budget. Romance may be a firm reality when it stands on the solid foundation of a businesslike management of financial affairs.

Money Is Not Everything

Among those higher financial brackets where the greatest percentage of conflict over money shows up are to be found some of the happiest married people in the world. Such happiness may also be found in some marriages on the lowest-income levels. Scattered among the middle-income marriages are people who are in financial trouble and people who manage their money in such a way that it contributes to their romance. In all the research thus far there is no correlation between the amount of money people have and their happiness in marriage. Apparently money cannot buy romance, nor can a limited income keep it out. Important though ample funds and good management are, romance in marriage as far as money is concerned depends in the last analysis upon the attitude we take toward money. In our economic morality nearly everything is measured by the dollar sign and it is easy to develop the illusion that money is the most important thing in the world. But in marriage, at least, there are many other things more important.

The common virtues, such as faith, hope, charity, prudence, fortitude, temperance, justice, honesty, and courage, apparently have more to do with romance than money has. Ridicule of these functional necessities seems to be the characteristic attitude of the person who lacks them, but no amount of ridicule can compensate for them in marriage or in any other relationships. There does appear to be a correlation between them and happiness in marriage. If they are not there, no amount of money seems to be enough to make up for them.

The relation of money to romance in marriage seems to depend upon which is considered more important: personality characteristics which make for good relationships, or money and the things which money can buy. Money is necessary but its powers are limited. It is no substitute for tender affection freely given. It cannot buy trustworthiness. Those who depend upon money and the things which money can buy are helpless and hopeless when money is gone. Those who depend upon personal resources of the kind necessary to develop relationships through which we experience life's greatest possibilities may have romance with or without money. The seers of the ages have understood this truth only too well. Observation from scientific research today verifies the insight phrased centuries ago, "Better a dinner of herbs where love is, than a stalled ox and hate therewith."

CHAPTER SIX

A New Angle on the Eternal Triangle

If you ever walked by a bakery at eleven thirty in the morning the chances are that you were quite well aware of its presence. It may have taken some self-discipline to get by. But if you walked back right after lunch (depending on where you had lunch, of course) you probably did not notice it at all. At least those enticing aromas would not reach you with as powerful a pull as before lunch when you were hungry and susceptible. After lunch your hunger was satisfied, and you were less vulnerable. You may have been able to go by without throwing self-discipline into second gear.

Life Is Full of Hungers

In addition to our hunger for food we have other hungers which need satisfying. Some of them should be satisfied in marriage. If they are not, then we may have to throw self-discipline into second or low gear to keep from sneaking off after some enticing promise of satisfaction outside marriage. We all have hungers for love and appreciation, respect and consideration, intellectual as well as recreational companionship, thoughtfulness and common courtesy. And most people will steal if they get hungry enough.

The business man who takes his secretary out to lunch and says, "My wife doesn't understand me," may be, and is usually considered to be, a wolf; but in too many instances he is stating the plain, simple truth. He is hungry for whatever he wraps up in the word "understanding," and his wife cannot, or will not satisfy his hunger. He is therefore keenly aware of any woman who appeals to him as capable and willing to satisfy his hunger for "understanding."

A woman longs for some demonstration of affection which looks a little like that which her husband showed her before they were married. She wants to feel admired, and now and then adored. She is hungry for his arms around her and his lips which whisper that she is beautiful and lovely on occasions besides during their sexual embraces. If he is too busy with business, or too self-centered about his own concerns to sense his wife's hungers she may feel the tremendous power in another man's look which says that she is desirable for love. She may have to fight herself, as well as some handsome wolf, or some other woman's hungry husband to keep the triangle out of her marriage. The fight could be too long and too much. Or she might become so hungry that she goes hunting, struggling with fear and guilt, but driven by starvation.

Some of our resort centers are filled with people who are hungry for affection, who long for some show of esteem which seems genuine, and who would be extremely happy at some show of real faith and trust. A husband or a wife back home apparently knows nothing of the deep hungers that bedevil their mate who has become a seeker after happiness among the lights and music where the lonely gather in crowds. Or when such hunger is known and there is incapacity or unwillingness to help satisfy it, there may be a hopeless resignation to what is considered inevitable. Scandal and divorce burst from discovery and publicity about the desperate efforts of the lost and starving to find satisfaction in basic human relationships. Rape and murder sometimes have their ugly roots entangled in the snarl of dissatisfactions in marriages that have failed.

A wedding does not blind the people who go through it. A husband will be able to recognize another beautiful woman when he sees her. A wife can spot a "tall, dark and handsome" man who is not her husband anywhere within the horizon. Neither mate is supposed to give any indication of it, or even admit it to oneself lest it would somehow threaten the marriage. Where people are immature, it would do so. But a wedding de-sexes neither a man nor a woman. Each can feel the pull of sex appeal whenever any appealing person comes along. It does not usually happen to any threatening extent with newlyweds. Their relationship is so all-satisfying to them that there is little hunger. But in those marriages that have passed the newlywed stage, if relationships are not satisfying, hunger can be so great that the "eternal triangle" is a definite threat.

A Mutually Satisfying Relationship Is the Key to Marital Security

The best safeguard against the threat of a third person in marriage is the achievement of mutually satisfying relationships within the marriage. Those who suppose that either heaven or the law will hand them guaranteed protection against outside threat along with a wedding certificate may be in for a rude awakening from that romantic dream. Every person who marries brings his own peculiar individual differences to the union and whoever marries him will be possessed of another set of individual differences. These differences cause conflict which has to be worked out through adjustment. The fact that one is a man and the other a woman, insures enough difference to make adjustment a very important skill in marriage. Among all the individual differences brought to any marriage by any man or woman are a number of needs that might be called hungers. If a marriage is to be really successful and romance a certainty, the two persons in it must have a capacity and a willingness to try to fulfill these needs and satisfy these hungers for each other. In a sense marriage

James E. Clark

swings on two hinges, adjustment and fulfillment. People who are preoccupied with themselves, unable to sense the needs of the other, or unwilling to help satisfy them, are asking for an invasion of some third person and the development of the "eternal triangle" in their marriage.

Here is a marriage which is more satisfying to the husband than to the wife. She is a good housekeeper and takes care of the children well. She looks nice when he shows her off on Ladies' Night at the club. She is not extravagant and manages well. But she is lonely for want of love. He is much involved in his business, but after all he is giving her everything in the world, isn't he? Look at the beautiful home he has provided. Look at their friends who admire her and envy them their fine car and their vacations. Look at her wonderful children. What more could she want? After working hard all day for his wife and children, he wants to relax at home and read the paper. What is a man's home for, anyway? And he fixes everything around the house that goes wrong, so why should she complain about his spending so much time at his bench in the basement? He is happy, so why isn't she? The idea that he is not supplying the one thing that a woman needs more than any other thing just does not seem to occur to him.

When she tries to tell him in all the subtle ways women have developed across the centuries, and finally just plain comes right out and tells him, he is offended. He expects her to see evidence of his love in tons of coal he buys for the furnace, or in beefsteak he brings for dinner, or in a diamond-studded watch; but she wants to see it in an occasional bouquet of roses, or a box of candy, or some new lingerie which he has bought with proper self-consciousness. She wants some evidence of his love in his taking her out, not too seldom, among the noise and the lights. Above all, she wants to see it in his eyes and hear it in his voice. She might be a different woman if he would take her in his arms in the kitchen while she has flour on her hands, vanilla spilled on her apron, hair flying loose and distraction in her eyes, and tell her that nothing matters but that she is his wife and he loves her and, by golly, she is beautiful! He could catch her when everybody is ready for church and she least expects it—and she might remain breathless clear through the sermon. A little sudden expression of love by a man for his wife is in no way inconsistent with the worship of God their Maker.

A wife may not realize just how hungry she is when these little expressions of love and affection are missing, until she meets some total stranger on the Community Chest drive and his look sends shivers through her. She may not know it but she could be ripe for the sort of romantic flirtation that is an invitation to the triangle, and her husband would probably blame her although he may be chiefly responsible.

When a marriage is more satisfying to the wife than to the husband he may be the one who is saying to his secretary that his wife doesn't understand him. He has no complaint about her housekeeping. The chances are that she is all but perfect at that. Most of the time the women who fail in their personal relationship with a husband are nearly perfect as housekeepers. The best companions usually keep the house in such manner that it looks as if somebody lived there, and now and then as if a cyclone had been a recent visitor. But the hungry husband who has no complaint about his wife's home economic skills may be starving for lack of her skills in the department where you turn a house into a home. He may become a powder keg just waiting for some blond feminine match to strike fire—and the "eternal triangle" flames into being.

There Is No Substitute for Character

One of the most disturbing facts about our relationships is that no one person can ever completely satisfy all the needs of any other individual. Romantic love makes a couple think that they can do so. The many who are disillusioned about this notion prove the fact. When a couple approach marriage with romantic love that makes them feel they can completely satisfy each other, they are on a winding road with a bridge out and no warning signs that they can recognize.

Since it is impossible for each of us to satisfy all the needs of our married partner, each of us will have some unsatisfactions. Areas of unsatisfactions are hunger areas, and hunger areas are danger spots for the development of the "eternal triangle." There is no marriage without such danger spots. For this reason there can be no substitute for character in marriage. That sense of personal integrity which enables a person to make good a promise and be dependable, is foundation material for any marriage. A sense of values that enables a person to recognize the importance of trust and trustworthiness in personal loyalties is indispensable. There will be times when unsatisfied hungers clamor for satisfaction. Separation or illness, or whatever disrupts the normal rhythm of marriage may put strain on the "ties that bind." The "eternal triangle" is not so much of a threat when people believe in each other because they can believe in themselves.

A woman in her forties fell in love with a man she met on a committee that was set up to plan a series of community musical events. She was the mother of three children and the wife of a prominent business man in the town. Both husband and wife belonged to a church and could be counted on for support of any worthwhile enterprise. They did many things together and enjoyed themselves as a family. They were happily married, as they looked at their marriage and as the community looked at it.

When this new love developed the wife was thrown into considerable agitation and confusion. She still loved her husband. She was bewildered partly because of her lack of knowledge that such a thing was possible. She felt terribly guilty and lay awake nights struggling with inner conflicts. Her pain was increased by the belief that love is a sign for marriage only. She wondered if her marriage was a mistake, yet much in her relations with her husband was sat-isfying, and she loved her children dearly. She sim-ply could not understand how it was possible for her to feel as she did about her family and this other man. She suffered for weeks and finally sought help from a marriage counselor. She made sure that he was dependable by writing the American Association of Marriage Counselors for information about whom she might see in her section of the country. (She had read about people who, claiming to be marriage counselors, were not adequately trained, and there-fore sometimes damaged marriage relationships more than they helped.)

During the course of her talks with the marriage counselor she became more aware of the real reasons for her feelings. She learned which of her ideas were just romantic illusions, and which would lead toward real romance. She discovered that such attraction is normal, and gradually realized that she had been mildly attracted to other men before this experi-ence, though she had never admitted it to herself. As the talks proceeded she began to feel relieved from the intensity of her conflict, and to work herself out of her mixed-up condition. She realized that she was not such a terrible person as she had thought and she became more sure of herself. She continued on the committee and experienced a gradual change of feel-ings toward the man. Later she remarked that it all seemed just like a dream. She wondered how she could have ever felt toward him as she did.

Through it all she stuck to her promises made

when she and her husband committed themselves to each other before God and those many witnesses. She held on to her loyalty by sheer strength of character. She used her head when she sought help from a skilled counselor about the sort of private family matter that people usually keep to themselves or seek advice about on grounds of friendship, not on grounds of adequate preparation to give the advice. She said afterward that it finally occurred to her that it was as sensible to consult a marriage counselor when her marriage was ill, as to go to a doctor when her body was ill.

Her husband knew that something severe was threatening her, but gave her support in his love and reassurance that she could handle whatever it was that bothered her. The children were aware that "mother is off the beam" for some reason. Friends knew that she was disturbed, but she did not make the mistake of confiding in her best friend who she knew would not have breathed a word about it. The man who was apparently causing all the trouble did not understand her embarrassment and self-consciousness in his presence, and interpreted her interest as enthusiasm for the musical programs they were planning.

Her marriage is a better marriage because of her experience. She is a more ardent wife and a more understanding mother as she contributes toward the preparation of her children for their marriages, years later. She is a much happier person with less fear of the future because of her insights and the strengths gained through her struggle. She won, where others have been hoodwinked by romantic illusion and tripped by immaturity into breaking up one marriage and falling into the trap of a new marriage that would have little chance of being half so satisfying as the first. She was threatened by lack of knowledge, painfully groping where she needed understanding, shaken by stormy emotions of fear and guilt, and pushed around by romantic ideas of love; but she hung on to her promises and came out on top. The muscles of her morality proved to be strong enough to hold while she used her intelligence. She now knows romance to a measure that is all too scarce among marriages.

Is Platonic Love the Answer?

Among the various choices facing the woman mentioned above was the choice of entering a mild flirtation, or a Platonic relationship. She said she decided against that because she knew she would be playing with fire. She was suspicious of Platonic love on the basis of her observations among her friends. Platonic love, as most people speak of it, is love without sex and without responsibilities. Most of us, when sex is mentioned, can think only of genital sex, or some physical sex act, but there is much more to sex than physiology. Sex colors the thinking and feeling of every person. We are not generally aware of the ways in which it is present in all our relationships. We are shocked when we are informed that sex is in father-daughter or mother-son relationships. We are so limited in our understanding of sex that we can think only in terms of actions leading up to or including sexual intercourse, unthinkable in parent-child relationships. We say, therefore, that there is no sex in such family relationships, or in friendships that do not include such acts.

When men deal with men in any way the masculine sex is dealing with the masculine sex. When women have anything to do with other women the feminine sex is having to do with the feminine sex. When a man and a woman look at each other, or engage in conversation on the telephone though hundreds of miles separate them, the masculine sex is looking at, or speaking to the feminine sex. There need not be any actions that fit our limited concepts of sex, but in the case of hungry people there may be. When people are starving for love, or understanding, it is pretty difficult to keep sex out. The loneliness which initiates Platonic relationships is evidence of hunger for more intimate communication. Sexual intercourse is the most intimate form of communication of which we humans are capable.

When a husband or wife enters what they call a Platonic relationship with someone outside their marriage it strongly suggests hunger resulting from dissatisfaction, or unsatisfaction, within the marriage. They expect to go further into intimate companionship than in ordinary friendship, although at least one and perhaps both do not expect "sex to rear its ugly head." In any case such a husband or wife is opening the door to the "eternal triangle." In such instances the married person may seem to love husband or wife even more, but that suggests compensation for guilt feeling. The story of the man who brought his wife a lavish present only to have her inquire, "What have you been up to now?" could easily apply here. Some Platonic relationships are broken up when the dangers of increasing intimacies are recognized. Some break up marriage. Romance is broken in either case.

Friendships do not have to threaten marriage; sometimes they enrich and support. Most friendships exist without any realization of the sex elements in them; but when friendships are allowed to cross the lines of intimacy which should be reserved for marriage, sex crosses the lines too, in erotic imaginations, in substitute images during intercourse with the marriage partner, or in actual illicit affairs.

Not long ago two married couples became greatly attached to each other. They were together continually and enjoyed each other's company very much. Their friendship was most satisfying. They visited in each other's homes until everyone felt almost as much at home in the other's house as in his own. Some of the bars of privacy were gradually let down. Nobody meant any harm but everybody became more intimate. A "very close friendship" developed between one of the men and the other man's wife. They referred to it as their Platonic friendship. All parties tried to act as if it were perfectly justified and anyone who questioned it was certainly a "prude," not quite mature. Finally, however, there were words about it in one of the marriages and that conflict forced the couple underground.

"He" began to drop around when her husband was away. It was not long before they were caught in the rapids of a sex-loaded love which they interpreted as "we were really meant for each other," and with such a love as theirs, "it must be God's will." It was too late for the brakes. Two marriages crashed and the ambulance of divorce picked up the smashed people. Rumor damaged reputation and business. The "innocent parties" moved away, but the Platonic friends married. They are having a hard time proving to themselves and everybody else that they are happily married. Each has proof of what the other is capable of doing with a close friendship, and both are afraid to develop new friendships. This second marriage is not so satisfying as the first to either of them, and both are thinking of divorce again. What they thought was romance proved only romantic illusion leading to the "eternal triangle."

When separation is forced upon a couple by business, or war, or whatever, if it is a long separation, there is risk of the crawling approach of the triangle. Hungers heretofore satisfied are left suddenly unsatisfied, or with substitutes. They may be increased because of the knowledge that they cannot be satisfied directly. How the person deals with these hungers may make all the difference as far as romance in marriage is concerned.

It is not easy to be the odd one in a group of people all of whom are married, including yourself, but with everybody else having a husband or wife within reach. There is not only the problem of one's own hungers; if the odd one is a woman some men seem to think both that she is starving and that she will welcome just the sort of satisfactions they can give in some other way than like long-lost brothers. She has the ticklish problem of seeking companionship to assuage her own hungers somewhat, at the same time being careful not to walk into some marital pasture and wave a red flag in front of the bull! She may find the wives of all handy husbands suddenly mistrusting her, and overdoing themselves to be nice to her. It is not easy, but she will have to adjust otherwise than by a Platonic relationship or an admittedly illicit affair. Romance is not acquired by theft, nor is it nourished by destroying the romance of others.

If the odd one is a married man he may have similar battles because of female wolves in wives' clothing. Men do not have any option on sexual exploitation, and not all "gold diggers" are unmarried. He will have his own hungers to deal with, and some innocent wife with hungers of her own may feel sorry for him, and want to help assuage his loneliness out of supposedly pure sympathy or just a strong mothering urge. If he follows the all too prevalent masculine line of reasoning he may erroneously judge himself free to seek companionship, including sex, at will. Men have assumed the right of sexual exploitation of the female for centuries. A certain social attitude still makes the only undesirable consequence that of being caught. Another undesirable consequence, however, over which social attitude seems to exercise little control is the destruction of romance. There are men who stand separation from their wives for several war years and come home with personal integrity intact and a much better chance for romance in their marriage.

Those who have been swept by romantic love into marriage that is dangerously unsatisfying, and those who frequently feel hunger for a more abundant companionship even when the marriage is basically satisfying, can increase romance in their marriage. They must realize that the best safeguard against the threat of the third person and the pain of the "eternal triangle" is the development of the most mutually satisfying relationship. When prolonged separation is forced upon them they must seek satisfactions which are not likely to invite invasion of the marriage. Since all perfect marriages exist—if they exist at all—in heaven, there will be some hungers for all of us along this earthly marital trail. When hunger is strong and direct satisfaction is impossible, nothing but character can protect the chances of romance. Romance is not child's play; it is not even adolescent fun. It is for maturing adults, and one sign of maturity is moral integrity. It is being proved all around us. Romantic indigestion is the price for undisciplined satisfaction of hungers outside marriage, which should find appeasement through a balanced diet of mutual satisfaction prepared with love in the romance of home.

CHAPTER SEVEN

Immaturity—A Killer of Romance

The greatest threat to romance in marriage is immaturity. There are too many child marriages. This declaration has no reference to people who marry at fourteen or fifteen years of age, but to older people who have never grown up. When adults enter marriage with childish resources there is little chance for romance, no matter how romantic they were in their approach to marriage.

What Is Maturity?

"Maturity" is a term that has been used in a variety of ways. For our purposes we shall interpret it to mean the full development of all resources to capacity for any age. A three-year-old child may be mature if all its resources are developed as much as they could be in three years. A thirty-year-old person would be mature if all resources of body and mind and spirit were developed to full capacity for thirty years.

It is readily observable, however, that nobody develops all his resources to full capacity at any time. Nor do we develop all our resources at the same time or at the same rate. We can spurt ahead in physical growth during adolescence and lag behind in mental development. As adults we could be about average in mental growth and lag behind spiritually. Maturity in a ten-year-old might be immaturity in a person fifteen years of age. A child of four may throw a tantrum and be mature for a four-year-old, but a person of twenty-four who throws a tantrum is clearly immature if that is his usual way of reacting to frustration. By twenty-four temper should have been disciplined enough to keep it from getting completely out of control. A person should have learned how to direct it in ways that would help instead of letting it run amuck and defeat his own purposes.

Temper

Each age makes its own demands. Maturity at thirty is much more demanding than maturity at twenty. Fifty requires considerably more maturity than thirty. Growth is always in process, or at least should continue as the years pass. Because growth is always in process there can be no fully mature people, but there are some people more mature than others. Some are so immature, even though they have become adults, that they have a terrible time with life. Married people have sent romance flying out the window when one or the other was unable to deal with adjustment problems as a maturing adult, and could act only like a child.

The Signs of Immaturity Are Recognizable

The signs of immaturity are more easily recognizable than the characteristics of maturity. We see more of them. If we can identify them as evidences of immaturity, and realize how they threaten marriage and romance in marriage we may be able to understand better what maturity is and how to attain it. The pay-off will be worth the struggle. We shall take the average age for marriage as our measuring point and shall consider maturity for men and women around the ages of twenty-five and twenty-three.

A certain young woman was very easily influenced by her friends. She seemed unable to make up her mind by herself. She was always asking someone what to do whenever she had to make a decision. When she married she depended too much upon her husband. Perhaps her parents made her decisions for her long after she should have been making them for herself. Whatever the cause, she was helpless when she had to decide about anything. At first her husband thought it was wonderful to have her so completely dependent upon him, but after a while he became impatient. By our measurement age, or the average age for marriage, she should have been able to make up her mind for herself. In doing so, she would have taken other people and things into account in doing it but she would not let others exercise too much influence.

Whenever a certain man was faced with problems

he would come up with ready-made answers from his store of preconceived ideas or opinions. Even he did not know where he got them, but since they were his, by adoption or otherwise, they should work. But they did not always solve his problems. He had never learned to think in an effort to understand the nature of any given problem, and did not know that solutions tend to emerge from the understanding of the problem. He was always looking for answers ready-made. When he asked for help it was always in the form of advice. What he needed was somebody to help him learn to think, not somebody to solve his problems for him. Married people who strive to understand the nature of their difficulties, instead of only arguing about them, usually work things out.

[handwritten margin note: Understand nature of problem]

Every neighborhood has someone who seems to think that everyone else should do the adjusting. They have had their way so long, or their need to dominate is so strong, that they seem to think everyone should cater to them. In successful marriages each partner is mature enough to take the initiative in seeking to adjust most of the time. The old idea that marriage is a "50-50" proposition is misleading. In most marriages somebody has to make it 60-40 now and then, or 90-10. Sometimes it has to be 101-0. The people who are constantly watching to see whether the other one is delivering his full 50 per cent, and being very careful to supply his own but no more, are likely to miss the real wonder of ro-

[handwritten margin note: No 50-50 for adjustment]

mance. You find most romance in marriages where people are trying to see who can go the furthest.

A child, because he is a child, is so self-centered that he may rush through the living room when company is present, as if nobody were within a thousand miles. The child does not mean to offend. He is so wrapped up in what he wants that he does not know he may have offended. Being a child he has not had time enough to learn and practice good manners equal to the requirements of adults. As he grows up, unless he is merely taught to perform, he may learn about the rights of others and how to respect them. He will then show consideration instead of giving offense. If a person marries before that much maturity has been reached, marriage can be rough! He may be on the road to losing friends because of the way he influences people. He might lose his closest friend, the one he married.

Easily hurt

It is true that some people seem almost immune to offense. Their feelings are not easily hurt. They are a great pleasure to have around and easy to live with. Some folks, in contrast, are so touchy that you never know when they are going to be hurt. They take offense at the most unexpected times and to everyone's surprise. They deserve our sympathy, for they feel so inferior and insecure that they are always watching for signs that others see their inferiority. They are so self-conscious about it that they may interpret almost anything as proof that someone thinks them inferior or feels superior to them, and so take offense. You walk on eggs around them and keep your fingers crossed. You try to be ready for some sudden martyred withdrawal or angry attack, but you are never ready. A child can't have all the candy it wants, so it won't have any. You don't pay enough attention to it, so it won't play. Occasionally a married couple are barred from romance because one or the other is suddenly offended and wants to pick up his dolls and go home. Some people pick up suitcases and go. They should! Home is where they belong until they grow up.

There is a wife in a certain community who turns on the waterworks whenever she wants anything. Crying was successful with her father and it works with her husband. It could be that she picked him because of that. Anyway, if it did not work she would not cry. Her husband could help her to grow up if he would just let her drain the reservoir. But there is supposed to be something unmanly about letting a woman cry, especially your wife. Of course, there is nothing unwomanly about a woman's crying, even if she uses that method to get what she wants like a child!

crying to get what they want

Some men use the same principle. They do not cry, but they storm and howl and threaten to tear the roof off. It worked with mother and it works with the little wife. If he does not storm he may pout or sulk. Wives can get good at this, too. But the star performer in the immaturity circus is the person who always has something out of the past to throw up to

storming to get what they want

skeletons in closet

the other when they get into a dead end argument. Such a performance by an adult looks amusing to an outsider, but there is nothing funny about what it can do to romance in marriage.

Affection Can Be Misused as Bribery

Here is a woman who gets her way by swamping her husband with affection. She wrapped her daddy around her little finger with it, and that form of bribery is effective with some husbands, too. Some women use sex by actually bargaining with it. Many a man has been whipped into line, or over the line into some other woman's arms, by this powerful feminine weapon. A pregnant woman obtained a fur coat by threatening to harm herself and her unborn child. The fact that medical care and hospitalization were threatened financially made no difference to her. She wanted what she wanted when she wanted it, and she discovered that she held a powerful weapon in her pregnancy. Such action is clear evidence of immaturity, and the fact that a person is twenty-four, or thirty-six, would not change it. Romance cannot long stand that sort of whipping or bribery. This woman was a child in adult clothing. She now has a child and a fur coat—but no husband.

Occasionally you see a husband, or it might be a wife, who must always be the life of the party. You hear his voice above all the others. His laugh drowns out other sounds of merriment. If it is the wife, she may dress gaudily, and she may use cosmetics like flags in a parade. Such people have unusually strong needs for attention. The probabilities are that they did not receive enough attention when they were children, or they were given too much, and must continue to strive for it now that they are adults. A child may start showing off the minute company arrives. If he does not get attention immediately he may get noisy about it. He could get violent. He needs attention, and by all the goblins in Oz, he is going to get it somehow! His older brother or sister, now married, who acts that way apparently has the same childish need.

Most men need encouragement from their wives, but some men cannot produce unless they are constantly praised. They must have it from everybody. When properly supplied they function well. Blame and criticism throw them into the alibi-ing dumps. Children respond to praise and blame because their opinion of themselves depends upon the opinion of others around them. As a man grows up it is to be expected that he may develop a fair idea about his own strengths and weaknesses. He should be able to see how much praise he deserves and how much of the praise is flattery or overestimation. He ought to be able to understand whether blame is justified. *Praise & blame* There are women who flutter above the clouds on the wings of compliments, but are crushed to earth under the weight of criticism. When we are old enough for marriage we should be able to measure the judgments of others by an increasingly clear concept of ourselves, which is also increasingly accurate. Praise and blame should neither lift us too high nor throw us too hard.

Praising a little

Any marriage would improve if the husband could notice the little things about his wife that deserve praise, and mention them more often. It works both ways. Many a wife would be amazed at her husband's changed attitude toward her if she praised him in public, and in private, without stretching anything. There is something quite praiseworthy about any wife or husband if you look for it. Unfortunately, we have had more practice looking for something to complain about, and we are better at blame than at compliment; but roses are more conducive to romance in marriage—even verbal ones— than brickbats. Grown-up women could even praise other men's wives, and mean it.

Living up to mistakes by trying to correct them in reality rather than in Dreams.

When a man's actions at some party suggest the antics of a male donkey, and his wife, on the way home, is accurately descriptive about his behavior, he may prove his maturity by efforts to reduce the resemblance. But some men can respond only by retaliation in describing the wife at *her* worst and deliberately exaggerating the original resemblance at the next party. Another childish way to mishandle this problem is for the husband to dream up another party in which he is a perfect whatever-he-was-*not* at the last one. He could attempt to solve his problem in his imagination. A woman who has failed to achieve romance in her marriage may submerge herself in a sea of love stories which she finds in love-story magazines. Here she may have a substitute experience in romantic illusions, and may revel in romantic illegitimacies in which she would not dare indulge in real life. There are many ways of retreating into the unreal world to avoid dealing with problems in real life. The trouble is that people who retreat into a dream to handle life are doomed to experience romance only in a dream.

Illness Can Be Misused

Every doctor sees people who enjoy being ill. It could be a man but it is more frequently a woman. She exaggerates symptoms of whatever she thinks the trouble is. She picks something that will give her enough status and insure attention and sympathy. She may be a person who, no matter how bad your illness was, will claim that hers was ten times worse. She takes advantage of any little sore throat, sneeze, crick in her hip, or vague "not feeling well," and works it for all that it is worth. She is able to have a crick almost at will. If real illness comes along you would think that she was dying. She never has learned to accept illness for what it is and to get out of it as quickly as possible, because she needs it otherwise than for physical health. Little boys and girls can suffer with hurts and bruises that happened days ago and are long since healed, when there is sudden need for sympathy. It is not pleasant to live with such a child in marriage even if he does wear long pants, or if she has started signing her name with a Mrs. instead of a Miss. Romance is sickly and pale at best.

A husband who is not climbing the ladder of success as rapidly as he wants to and places blame on everything and everybody but himself is not exactly fascinating as a marriage partner. The wife who never can find time to do the hundreds of thousands of things she has to do simply because there is not enough time may be projecting blame in a vague sort of way. The need to project blame and alibi for failure is common among children. They are not big enough to accept responsibility for their own acts and the consequences, particularly when the consequences are threatening. They have to grow up and become strong in self-regard before they can "take it." Some people marry before they have grown up to that degree. For whatever happens that is not good, the other or the weather, or God, is always to blame.

The husband or wife who is always right is discomforting to romance in marriage. Apparently romance cannot live in such a rarefied atmosphere. Children, however, must always be right; it is necessary for their security. Those of us who have grown up can recall once when we were wrong, back about ten years somewhere. We know, therefore, that it is just barely possible that we may be wrong again sometime in the distant future. We hate to admit it, but we realize that we are not God, really, but human

[handwritten margin note: Projecting blame to other reasons than self]

[handwritten margin note: Being always right]

beings, with about their usual number of times of being right and wrong. It is a healthy marriage where a man can allow his wife to be right at least ten per cent of the time. A woman might be surprised, too, at her husband's noticing how bright she is if she lets him be right almost fifty per cent of the time.

Drinking May Substitute for Growth

Another sign of immaturity may be recognized when people gather for a social evening and have to drink in order to be sociable. Lacking in social ease we may use a substitute for growth in the form of liquor, an anesthetic depressant which may deaden our fear of our inadequacy and make us bold enough to be an enjoyable person until the reaction sets in. There are many reasons for drinking, but we are discussing the ones which root in immaturity. When people succumb to social pressure against better judgment immaturity is suggested. It is suggested when people dare not entertain without cocktails for fear of what people may say who think that in order to be anybody you must serve liquor. Their need to belong and be accepted is compulsively strong, therefore they will conform, even though they hate the stuff. The immature among those who attend dare not refuse because drinking has become the mark of sophistication and they feel that they must prove themselves sophisticated. Some adult groups can take the very things which prove them childish and make them measurements of maturity as far as the group is concerned.

The person who drinks to escape from the necessity of dealing with frustration or crisis is trying the childish way of evasion. People who try to drown guilt feelings, a sense of inadequacy, feelings of defeat, and the like in drinking are showing immaturity. A person who becomes bewildered or anxious about a marriage which seems to be falling to pieces and takes to drink will speed the fall. The marriage in which either husband or wife uses liquor as a substitute for growth is a risky marriage. No amount of liquor ever brought about good adjustments in marriage, but it can be found frequently among the ruins of broken marriages.

It would be inaccurate to suppose that everyone who uses liquor is immature. Some of those who fight liquor most have demonstrated immaturity in their attitudes and methods. Liquor may be considered in somewhat the same manner as sex and fire in previous discussion as far as its use is concerned. Given enough knowledge and understanding, sufficient respectful carefulness, and there need be no stark tragedy. Put liquor into the hands of careless and immature people, and they can get hurt and hurt others. Witness the highway accident toll involving liquor, the rising rate of illegitimate parentage in which drink is a contributing factor, and the tax load for police and court action, which is a direct result of drinking.

"Piggy Back" Religion Shows Immaturity

Another sign of immaturity is revealed by the person who rides "piggy back" as far as religion and morality are concerned. As little children we needed parents to tell us what was right and what was wrong. When we grew up we began to understand the principles upon which right and wrong are decided, and we began to make our own decisions accordingly. We developed our own standards. But there are some people who claim to be very religious, and their religion consists of a list of do's and don'ts which they follow for fear of consequences. Their prayers are mostly "gimme's" and they usually take it upon themselves to tell the Lord what a mess his world is in. They are constantly asking the Lord to rearrange it according to their desire or for their special benefit. They believe the Bible "from cover to cover," with little idea of what is between the covers, or how it got there. They can quote Scripture by the yard, but they use only that which supports their ideas and opinions.

Religion in the hands of mature people can be a strong support in time of trouble. It can supply a light in the night of disillusionment and despair. It can be a source of power beyond human resources which may enable a person to turn tragedy into triumph. It can supply courage enough to live, not just courage enough to die. Religion for those who are growing up may involve the touch of the Spirit of

God in such manner as to direct growth toward the highest and best we know in personality. It can supply incentive for a continuing search for truth, courage enough to dare to face it, even in human relationships, especially those between a husband and a wife. Religion in the maturing can create a little bit of heaven here on earth. In the hands of the childish it can create a little hell in the here and now. Religion is not full of showers of blessings merely because you call it "religion." It may bless, but it may also curse, depending upon its nature and the maturity of the people when it enslaves or frees.

Snobbery Is a Sign of Immaturity

The person who marries a snob may find that life can be unbeautiful. Children are inferior when measured by the adult world into which they are born. Because they are inferior they need to feel superior. While they are children they will try to even things up by making claims to feats far beyond their abilities. They commonly make claims for their family or friends which represent a slight exaggeration. They sometimes belittle other children in order to bolster their own status. When children become adults, those who do not grow up will continue the process of bolstering themselves. They will imitate people whom they recognize as superior and spurn those whom they consider inferior. The snob frequently attempts to secure a sense of superiority by talking other people down, by belittling, or by other methods of trampling in order to climb.

Few Women Can Grow Old Gracefully

One of the clearest signs of immaturity is the inability to accept the inevitable without feeling defeated. Few women can grow old gracefully. The advertisers and the movies have succeeded so well in making the adolescent girl a powerful ideal that literally thousands of women strain in desperation to look and act like adolescents all their lives. The standard is fixed so firmly that men in general tend to place highest premium on feminine personal appearance of the type which is crowded into a very few years in any woman's life. Too much attention is given to the outward appearance of the person rather than to the personality. The wrappings seem to be much more important than the contents of the package. In women who no longer mention their age, adolescent looks are possible only through imitation and the art of camouflage. The idea of a middle-aged woman's being beautiful if she looks like a middle-aged woman is preposterous to them. The very term "middle-aged" is downright repulsive to most women.

This distorted idea, among the mess of misleading romantic ideas, has so thoroughly threatened and warped the lives of some women that envy and jealousy cause conflict between many mothers and their late teen-age daughters. Watch how fiercely a woman will mistreat her body by misguided dieting, or violent exercise, in order to whip it into some semblance of comparison with that of her youthful offspring. Look at the smiling viciousness with which some women battle in efforts to prove that they have found the fountain of eternal youth. If a woman decides to give up the unnatural struggle she frequently over-does her nonchalance in proof of her hidden feelings of self-depreciation.

There is, of course, no excuse for sloppiness in looks or body condition. Maturity is not proved by transplanted "Bohemianism" masquerading as "don't-care-ness." There is much to be said for a discipline which avoids let-down or excess. But the abnormal struggle of many women to make their appearance at forty fit that of a woman of twenty *is* excess. A woman can be beautiful at fifty, by standards appropriate to the age of fifty, but not so long as the standard for twenty is the only standard there is.

Maturity is acquired through the development of resources appropriate to one's age, not through efforts to stop time, hold back the years, and arrest development at the point of late adolescence. It is a cruel, false ideal, and women beyond the twenties pay a terrible price for it all the rest of their lives. Only romantic froth is possible in a marriage where a woman must be forever striving to fool herself and her friends by attempting to reproduce the past instead of using to their fullest her resources of the present. Romance does not rest upon such flimsy supports as a girlish figure. It stands solidly upon the personality of the maturing woman who is, as a person, beautiful.

Finally, the husband or wife who thinks that he or she has arrived at full maturity is showing the clearest sign of immaturity. The ability to appraise oneself correctly is a sign of maturity, and any correct appraisal will show anyone ways in which he may continue to grow with benefit. It is a pleasure to live with someone who is aware that he falls a little short of the ultimate. He could agree, with a grin, after some foolish stunt, that it was a little childish, after all. You could forgive him with a feeling of gratitude in your heart that you had married a grown man. The really mature person will walk up in front of a mirror of personality now and then to see where improvement might still be made.

[margin note: Thinking you are at full maturity.]

One of the most difficult things about trying to live with a person who thinks himself fully mature is the problem of resisting politely the numerous and persistent efforts he makes to change you into the sort of person which obviously you are not but certainly ought to be. He works at it with all the zeal of the missionary. Romance could not possibly live in such a marriage because the zealot would have to be forever nagging it toward perfection too.

[margin note: changing the other person]

Caution: Don't Jump to Conclusions!

It should be pointed out that immaturity does not always mean that a person is acting like a child. When a forty-year-old acts like twenty, or a seventy-year-old acts like forty it may mean immaturity. When any resource lags behind very far it could mean immaturity as far as that particular resource is concerned. But any one of the signs of immaturity discussed in this chapter, by itself, does not necessarily mean immaturity. Some of the signs described could be caused on occasion by indigestion, or where you were last night, or how things are going at the office lately, or the time of the month in relation to a menstrual cycle. But if a person shows several of these signs in his behavior nearly all the time, immaturity is a good bet.

People have been hurt by jumping to conclusions about themselves and other people. If you can hold judgment until you have time to examine further, to observe and contemplate, you may arrive at a more nearly valid conclusion. Maturity or immaturity does not hang on a single word, or on one evening's performance. It shows up as characteristic behavior through months or years.

When you boil it down, maturity looks something like the following: A mature person can control his temper, at least most of the time. Mature persons make up their minds by the process of independent thinking, not by impulse or emotion. They do not look for answers but try to think things through in an effort to understand, and they usually find solutions emerging through their understanding. If they do not see all the angles they will seek counsel from some competent source of help. Mature people take

the initiative in making adjustments. They are likely
to prove their respect and esteem by attitudes and
actions when they deal with others.

Mature persons use tact and persuasion and are
not easily offended. They co-operate and enjoy participation in a group without always having to have
the spotlight. They have learned to sprinkle a little
salt on both praise and blame before they taste it.
They notice and remark about the admirable in their
marriage partner. They work together on their problems without going up like volcanoes, or acting as if
the problem did not exist, or skidding off into the
dream world to solve them. They can take illness
quietly and come out of it without headlines and a
brass band. They are quite ready to admit mistakes,
when they recognize them, and are usually able to
learn through the experience. They drink, if they
drink at all, for sociability, rather than because they
think they have to in order to belong, or to evade
some issue, or to compensate for some weakness.
They have their own set of standards, the function
of which they understand well enough to explain
"why" to their children.

Mature people are concerned about religion as one
of the ways of discovering truth, and as a guide for
the integration of life around values which are derived from their concept of the Divine. They have
confidence in themselves and other people, especially
their marriage partner. They are working for success
in the present and are not griping about an unattain-

able future, or coasting on achievements of the past. They are happy and content to make the most of the years, keeping themselves "handsome" and "beautiful" as handsome is and beauty does, according to the measure of their age. They are aware of ways in which they might still grow and are working at it.

The signs described in this chapter are not all the signs of maturity or immaturity which exist, but they represent the sort of attitudes and behavior, some of the ways people act and think, when they have not yet grown up enough for marriage, or enough to make romance possible in marriage. Immaturity kills romance. Maturity builds it. But remember, romance wasn't built in a day!

CHAPTER EIGHT

The Relation of Freedom to Romance

The custom of the stag party for the groom on the eve of the wedding is not so much a celebration of joy over the new freedoms which this fortunate man is acquiring, as a last-fling fond adieu to the old freedoms which this unfortunate man is giving up. There is no such party for the bride. All her affairs are in celebration of the freedoms which she is gaining, with little regret for the freedoms which she is giving up. Even those parties called "showers" whereby she acquires a dowry at the expense of acquaintances point hopefully toward the future instead of regretfully toward the past. The husband and wife who find new freedom in their marriage find romance.

The man who refers to his wife as "the ball and chain" may be using a pet phrase which indicates his love for her, but he may be suggesting that he has not discovered the freedoms of marriage and is only too much aware of the "ties that bind." It is true that the partnership of marriage is entered by contract and that contracts are supposed to be binding, but it is also true that partnerships are entered to enable two persons to accomplish together what neither of them could accomplish separately. In that sense the marriage contract is freeing as well as binding. The successful achievement of whatever enterprise depends, in the last analysis, upon the degree to which each partner is free to contribute toward its accomplishment. Freedom to perform in any endeavor is determined by knowledge and skill.

The doctor is free to help people stay well or regain their health, in proportion to his knowledge and skill in the practice of medicine. The airplane pilot is free to accomplish thrilling take-offs and happy landings in accordance with his knowledge of aerodynamics and his skills in flying. The husband and wife are free to experience romance in marriage in proportion to their knowledge of human relations and their skills in applying it. An understanding of the nature and progress of the maturation process is of utmost importance, for it is only through continued growth that we may discover the new freedoms which expand romance in marriage.

Each of us lived most of his life before marriage in what has been termed an "I" frame of reference. It was revealed in the way we talked and most of our talk was self-centered. "I want," "I am going," "I need," are easily recalled samples, which persisted as we moved through childhood toward maturity. The "we" relationships which were provided by our family experiences, and fostered by our parents, pushed us toward that more mature frame of reference, but slowly and in conflict with the "I." If you draw a circle about an inch in diameter, and then another circle about a quarter of an inch in diameter within the larger one you can picture it. The larger circle represents the "I" interests and concerns. The "we" feelings are there but very small as compared with the "I."

As we grew up the "we" circle grew in size and the "I" circle diminished until they were nearly the same size. If we continued to grow toward the maturity of adulthood the "we" circle would become the larger. In marriage that is what should happen. Evidence that it has happened or is happening may be seen in the refusal of one to make decisions involving both without talking things over before a decision is reached. A joint banking account where both husband and wife check on it suggests freedom not present in those marriages where money is exclusively in the hands of the husband and advanced at the embarrassed request or angry demand of the wife.

The wife who is competent in handling money demonstrates skill and ability through which the freedom of a joint checking account may be achieved. The husband who is freed from the masculine superiority complex may demonstrate that he has grown beyond the idea of "my" marriage and "my" money and has recognized that it is "our" in both cases. If there is no attitude of dominance and submission, a system may be established whereby only one person writes the checks, and yet both feel the relaxed freedom which is possible when dependence is only a foundation for independence.

Fortunately quite a number of husbands do not need to be mothered by their wives all the time. And just as fortunately quite a number of wives do not need a husband to take care of them as their father did. Such married people have acquired an independence which makes greater freedom possible. They are aware of the responsibilities of fidelity and by living in harmony with these responsibilities they gain the freedom from fear which makes trust possible. They have developed the habit of taking each other into account, not as a restraining influence, but as a person for whom they want to live, and for whose happiness they want to give themselves. It makes them happy to make others happy, especially the one in the marriage relationship with them.

Freedom Is Related to Maturity

When we left our childhood home we faced a situation which demanded more of us. We were limited by our unfamiliarity with surroundings, the strangers among whom we had to find friends, responsibility to do for ourselves whatever our parents did for us up to the time we ventured on our own. We were faced with challenge. We had to extend ourselves to become familiar with surroundings, and to get acquainted with people. We had, somehow, to handle whatever problems arose. And for every one of us there were moments when we wished we were back where everything was familiar. We longed to see faces we had known for years. We yearned for the safety and protection we had at home. It hit some of us hard enough to be called homesickness. It overpowered some persons here and there and they went home. It was a desire to run away from the more demanding situation and find sanctuary on a more immature level.

If we met the challenge through developing our resources of personality until we were equal to the demands, we continued to mature. We became more confident and less fearful of our adequacy. We developed strength in self-discipline beyond what we had previously. Additional knowledge gave increased understanding. We knew that we were progressing. We began to feel easier in our relationships and more at home in the new surroundings. We were gaining freedom from insecurity, uneasiness, and anxiety over whether we could make it. We were discovering freedom from worry over our acceptability among other people. We were finding freedom to enjoy our surroundings, the people with whom we worked, and the satisfactions of our own achievements. We were happy in these new and larger freedoms. But we acquired them through continuing to grow and mature.

Marriage offers an unusually fine opportunity for people to gain ever widening horizons of freedom. In committing themselves to each other two persons create new demands upon themselves. They must become reliable for two, not just for one. They must think and feel in terms of two, and before long, more than two, perhaps. They must plan for a long-term future, not just the foreseeable present. They must work out differences which cause conflict. They must adjust. They must manage their emotions well enough to keep from being overwhelmed by them. They must work and produce. If they are successful they develop their resources of personality, their skills of relationships toward greater maturity. They experience increasing freedom from suspicion, anxiety, worry, and fear. They acquire freedom from feelings of inferiority and inadequacy. They are released from frustrations which could result in virtual imprisonment of the spirit. They can be happy in the realization of a happy marriage. They will know romance.

The husband and wife who are maturing will work to reduce the ways in which they may compete. Instead of striving for the limelight they may direct attention toward the other. The wife who recognizes her husband's strong points and remarks about them in his presence when they are among friends may discover the freedom from need for attention herself. If her husband gives credit for her accomplishments supported by a tone of pride in his voice he may discover the freedoms which may be enjoyed when people do not need to compete. When married people are concerned to change themselves instead of the other one, if any change seems desirable, they are likely to experience the relieving freedom from nagging that is not possible to those who must make the other one over.

The maturing husband or wife is gaining in self-confidence and therefore does not have to compete to reassure. Such a married person is free from strains of guilt and the kind of anxiety which causes them to be forever testing in order to prove their adequacy. Such married people enjoy doing the job they must do in the division of labor in the marriage partnership, not only because of the personal satisfaction they may derive from it, but because of what it means to the other one. They become increasingly skilled in the fine art of co-operation. It is not an art which is easily learned and developed. Most of our childhood is spent in being competitive. All through school we are in more competitive than co-operative situations. Co-operation as an act, or a series of acts, is possible to children and youth, but co-operation as a way of life is possible only to the maturing on the adult level. Marriage provides excellent practice ground. A husband and wife may become as sure of themselves and each other as any team which achieves through highly developed co-operation. They will feel the freedom of working smoothly together toward common goals, and freedom from disappointment and bitterness which result from working at cross purposes, or selfishly toward the same goals.

Romance in marriage is increased through co-operation.

Conscience Should Free, Not Bind

If we were born into a family which recognized the value and importance of standards and ideals we were helped to form a conscience. As maturing adults we were then free from the pain and confusion of attempting to live our lives driven by impulse. Even the restraining function of conscience may contribute toward freedom from consequences of lack of restraint. If standards in our youth have been not too high, and ideals recognized as ideals, we are later free from the anxieties and frustrations, the blocks and inhibitions which stem from too severe or too harsh training. We are not haunted by fears and guilt which goad those who possess, or rather, are possessed by a diseased conscience. If parents were consistent in their assistance to us while we were developing our conscience we are free now from the bewilderment and confusion, the agony of indecision which characterize those whose guiding was less uniform.

As maturing adults, engaged in achieving a rich and abundant life through marriage, we can secure greater freedom and expand the horizons of romance by applying those maturing resources of mind to the re-examination of standards and the deeper perception of ideals. We can help each other to probe the meaning of morality and to modify our attitudes in relation to our understanding. We may strengthen conscience by freeing it from the chains of blind credulity and fanaticism and by nourishing it with knowledge, insight, and understanding gleaned from science and religion. The married couple who are maturing in their spiritual life beyond the fears and competitiveness of infancy and childhood may find abundant new freedoms through loving co-operation in efforts to know God's truths and to live life accordingly.

An immature conscience functions mainly as restraint and it is grounded upon a negative approach to the ideal. Fear provides its power. A maturing conscience functions as release and is grounded upon a positive approach to the ideal. Love provides its power. The mature conscience will restrain that which is hateful and destructive in human relations, including those referred to as marriage, but it will release and encourage that which is loving and beneficial, with greater emphasis upon the latter. Such a conscience would cause a married person, and any other, to be less concerned with what he should not do, and more concerned with what he should do. A person with such a conscience would become increasingly free in loving service to husband or wife and children, and that portion of the rest of the human race reached by their influence.

Freedom Is Relative

We may be able to gain greater freedom if we understand some of the "ifs" upon which freedom depends.

We are free to read French *if* we understand the French language. We are free to cross a river *if* there is a bridge, or a boat, or *if* we can swim. We are free to trust *if* we are not full of distrust. We are free to be satisfied and happy *if* we do not fail in adjustments and become angry, cruel, and hateful. We are free to love ourselves *if* we are doing all right in our dealing with all the many problems that make up our world; otherwise we probably shall not like ourselves. We are free to love another *if* we have grown up enough for our major concern to shift from ourselves to others. We are free to give attention, admiration, recognition, and regard to others *if* we have secured enough of these considerations across the childhood years and do not need to be forever striving for them ourselves.

Marriage offers opportunity for two persons who love each other to come to a better understanding of themselves and each other, and to help in the struggle for freedom. Married people may help each other to strengthen trust, to reduce anger and belligerency by co-operating to reduce friction. The husband and wife who talk over personal as well as mutual problems with each other may contribute toward greater understanding and solution of perplexing problems. Marriage may offer the chance for two persons to become so successful with "the hard realities of life" that they do not need the fanciful romantic unrealities of imagination. But romance in marriage depends upon the same "ifs" upon which freedom depends. Apparently both freedom and romance are related to the degree of achievement toward maturity and successful marriage. Knowledge and skill seem to be related to the degree of achievement. Those married people who seek the one and strive to continue the development of the other are increasingly free to experience the romance of marriage.

Freedoms Differ in Kind

There is a freedom which we experience when we walk around on the earth. There is a freedom which we experience when we fly. They are not the same kinds of freedom, nor are they secured in the same ways. The amusing statement by the frightened traveler, "I would love to fly if I could just keep one foot on the ground," is, nevertheless, a revelation of a recognition of the irreconcilability of two different freedoms. We know this in some of the more obvious ways. We agree that we are free to be here, or there, but we are not free to be both here and there at the same time. Another saying which reveals our general grasp of the difference in freedoms is recognized in the assertion, "You can't have your cake and eat it, too."

We are not so clear, however, in our understanding of the freedoms that are appropriate to single life and those appropriate to marriage. Some people even go so far as to try to secure both at the same time. The results are usually disastrous. Some try to get the freedoms of marriage while they are still single, by living as if they were married. Some married people try to get the freedoms of single life by living as if they were not married. Life can get all fouled up by such attempts to get the most out of life.

The pilot who takes off successfully and flies with any freedom knows perfectly well that he must operate his plane while still on the ground according to conditions which govern freedom on the ground. He knows just as well that the instant his plane leaves the ground he must operate it in harmony with those conditions which determine freedom in the air. He is willing to trade those freedoms which operate so long as he is earthbound for those which operate the moment he is air-borne. He knows that he would get into serious trouble if he tried to mix them, or act in one place as if he were in the other.

Some people enter marriage knowing what freedoms to look for and trying to relate themselves to requirements to get them. They are ready and willing to trade freedoms of single life for those of marriage. They understand that they must know what is required for successful marriage if they are to achieve it, just as surely as the pilot understands that he must know the requirements for successful flight if he is to accomplish it. A jet airplane branch of the Air Force has realized this principle so well that it has as a motto, "What you don't know will kill you." The same thing might be said for marriage and romance in marriage. What you don't know will limit your freedom to have either, and may destroy both. The old quotation "Ye shall know the truth and the truth will make you free," states a principle which operates in marriage and in flying—and apparently everywhere else in human experience.

How Can One Get More Freedom?

The first step toward the accomplishment of more freedom is to increase one's knowledge of those conditions through which freedom is secured. That is what the Wright Brothers did in order to accomplish flight. That is what engineers have done in improving our ability to fly, all the way from the boxkite type of the first airplane to the jet-propelled luxury liners of the skyways. We gained freedom to fly in proportion to that part of the truth about flying which we came to know. The same observation can be made regarding our freedom from hunger and disease. We are desperately striving to discover the truth about cancer in order to get free from its devastating effects. In one study it was revealed that in a wealthy community in our nation 70 per cent of the children were suffering from malnutrition. Their mothers do not know the truth about nourishment for their own children, and they will gain freedom from malnutrition and its effects in proportion to how much and how soon they learn about nutrition.

There are many married people who have realized this fact with respect to their marriage. They are studying in groups, or seeking advice about the best books to study as a couple or individually, in order to know more about what is required for successful marriage. They realize that freedom to accomplish it and the greater freedoms available through it depend to a considerable degree upon how much of the truth they know.

Another condition for the increase of freedom is to be seen in one's ability to apply what one knows. Any skill requires practice for its development. We may be free from the incapacitations of ill health if we know the conditions for health and apply them. We may be free from the destroying effects of fear, anger, and hate if we know how to exercise faith, hope, and love. We may gain freedom from the frustrations and maladjustments revealed in conflict in marriage if we know how to go about making adjustments and work at it. We may gain the freedoms of a loving, producing, giving parent if we know the exercise needed to develop our resources of personality in order to become that sort of person, and if we exercise sufficiently. We could become sufficiently mature to realize the freedoms in the romance of life if our love expanded enough to take in the whole human race. We should be able to rejoice in those freedoms identifying us with all human beings and sweeping us outward into the great stream that flows toward the Divine and generates the power needed to develop the Brotherhood of Man.

CHAPTER NINE

The Romance of Parenthood

The word "pioneer" suggests romance. It conjures up mental pictures of venturing into the unknown. All of us have listened with fascination to stories of the great adventurers in history, yet our day is an era of trail blazers, too. We have explored so many unknowns, discovered such startling new knowledge, and produced such astounding results that we call our day an age of miracles.

Most of these discoveries have been made in the universe outside of man, in the realm of material things. Some scientists think that the most amazing discoveries of the future will be made within man and his relationships, in the realm of the spiritual. Parenthood functions in the material and the spiritual realms, and some surprising discoveries have already been made which open up pioneering possibilities for modern parents.

In a sense, anyone who brings children into the world and attempts to "bring them up" is a pioneer, at least as far as his own parenthood is concerned. But fathers and mothers living today have a much

more exciting opportunity for exploration in parenthood than most of their predecessors. The borders of
the unknown are being pushed back, and the kind of
world for which we must help to prepare our children is radically different. There are at least three
areas where further exploration is essential, where
more knowledge is needed and where every parent
may pioneer.

One great area is that of the unknown within
every parent. We need to understand ourselves better
as parents. There is the area of the unknown within
our children. We would benefit from a better knowledge of what children are like generally, and what
our own children are like as individuals. And there
is the breath-taking unknown in our rapidly changing world. We may be of more real help to our children if we can understand the sort of world for which
we want to help them to prepare. The modern job
of parenthood requires an increasing amount of insight and understanding, of knowledge and skill; and
many parents are realizing it.

The time may come when parenthood will rank
among the top professions in the world. It may be
rated the most important when judged by the value
of its product. Certain individuals with insight have
held this to be true many times throughout history.
The emotional have sentimentalized about it. The
intellectual have said something like this, "Children
are not the hope of the world. Adults, in their dealing with children, are the hope or the despair of to-

morrow." Today, literally thousands of parents feel that their preparation for the job has been inadequate and so they are doing something about it.

Proof is seen in expanding research directed toward understanding children and parents, the relation of the childhood years to adult experiences, and the nature and rate of the maturation process. Additional proof is evident in the many local and national organizations and agencies through which modern parents are considering the findings from research, weighing and measuring them against their own experiences, and working to improve their parenthood. The time is not distant when the schools will provide better preparation for this greatest of all responsibilities, as an integrated plan within the curriculum. In the meantime, those of us who are parents, or who plan to be, may gain confidence through efforts to understand ourselves.

We Need to Understand Ourselves as Parents

Most of us have rejected the idea of bringing up our children "by the book," but not many of us today are willing to trust entirely to "common sense." Some of us have discovered errors in some "common sense" and we are glad to see modern psychology beat the fallacy out of it. Then others of us have recognized so-called "common sense" as little more than "what I already believe, stated in the way I'm used to hearing it said," without much regard for where it came from or whether it is valid. When we examined ourselves, some of us discovered that we thought our own brand of "common sense" was true, on no other grounds than that it was what we believed. Our believing it was sufficient to make it true, we thought. But more objective measurements are now available, and we can check our preconceptions against an increasing store of "the facts." The modern parent who is wise does not pitch out "common sense" merely because some error has been discovered in it. That would be like throwing out the proverbial baby with the bath. He just does not depend entirely upon "common sense."

Some of our parents have been greatly troubled by some of the disclosures from research and the pronouncements from "authorities." Before the magnitude of our task, and with growing realization of our lack of preparation for it, we have begun to feel somewhat hopeless and helpless. But most of us have determined to find out what we could and make the most of it. Some parents talk things over with other parents. It is helpful to look at common problems together. What happens depends upon the parents involved. A bit of knowledge may be handed on, but a pool of ignorance might be increased. The fact that others are facing the same sort of problems that we face may be comforting, but the fact that misery loves company does not necessarily contribute to the solution of any problem but the problem of loneliness.

Some parents come together in a group which

meets regularly and examines reports from sources recognized as more authoritative. Discussion based upon such reports is more likely to result in additional insights than discussions which are only an exchange of opinion. A "specialist" in some phase of parenthood may be invited to consult with the group, and much help may come from such consultation. Sometimes a neighbor passes on a book which was helpful, and some groups of parents have their own circulating libraries.

In looking into our personal parenthood we may discover why the best gift that we can give our children is a good marriage, our own. We may discover *why* the happiness of our own parents in their marriage did more toward insuring a happy childhood for us and providing good preparation for our marriage, than anything else. If our parents were unhappy we need to discover how we were affected, and how to modify those effects which are threats, in order to protect our children from them.

We are glad to discover how important our affection is to the security and growth of our children, and to find that we have an abundant supply of mature affection for them, if we have. But some of us learn with a shock that parents can seek revenge in dealing with their own children, for some treatment they received from their parents when they were children. We discover, with amazement, that it is possible for a parent to do this and not know that he is doing it. Learning how to realize when we may be doing it may improve our parenthood in its returns of romance to us and of happiness to our children.

Many fathers and mothers are learning how fatherhood and motherhood affect their relationships as husbands and wives. They are striving to understand and control their loves and their hates, their fears and their faiths, their trust and suspicion, their anger and their patience. They are trying because they know that their children will be exposed to all of it and be affected by it. They understand that the emotional atmosphere which they create will have more profound effect upon their children than any efforts at teaching or training which they make directly.

Some husbands have acquired sufficient insight to avoid feeling resentful toward wives who have become mothers and must give some of their time to it. These fathers are saved from the disquieting feelings of jealousy aroused in many fathers by a child who now demands much time and attention from his wife. Some wives are becoming better prepared to adjust the conflict between their role as wife and their role as mother, without serious loss to either. They know that it is not easy to whistle back a husband who has been lost because of the wife's preoccupation with motherhood.

Some wives understand that motherhood may be sought as an escape from the responsibilities of wifehood, or in compensation for failure as a wife. And so they safeguard both the romance of their marriage and that of their parenthood by working to achieve as wife and mother. Some fathers are beginning to understand that preoccupation with business, no matter how well rationalized as necessary to family welfare, may actually be escape from the responsibilities of fatherhood, or compensation for failure as a husband. These fathers, too, contribute to romance by working to adjust their conflicting roles.

There are mothers who, having heard that it is possible for them either to be of invaluable help to their sons or to cause irreparable damage by misguided mothering, are studying to discover how to be of most help. There are fathers, too, who realize that their relations with their very young daughters will result in either women who have grown up and are capable of giving and receiving love, or women who desperately need love but who are incapable of receiving it when it is offered. Some men and women understand that a wife may be expressing unconscious gratitude toward her father in her relationships with her husband, or seeking revenge upon her father in her treatment of her husband. Some husbands are pouring appreciation for their mothers into their relations with their wives, while others are punishing their mothers by making their wives miserable.

Through increasing self-understanding many modern parents are becoming more sure of themselves, and of more help to their children. Because of this growing insight into themselves these parents can permit their children to love abundantly and hate intensely, to laugh with abandon and explode in anger, and evaluate their experiences for themselves. Parents who know enough about themselves to be conscious of strengths and weaknesses, usually develop a tolerance of themselves which makes it easy for them to be tolerant with their children. Home is a place where children can be their worst selves as well as their best selves within the security of understanding parental affection, possible only to parents who understand themselves and like themselves. Apparently the better we understand ourselves as parents the more likely we are to understand our children as children.

We Need to Understand Our Children

Modern parents are more likely to relax when children are being children because they understand that "children are like that." They have heard of "ages and stages" and are not bothered by erroneous ideas of what children are and how they should act. Their children are not hounded by parents who are forever bedeviling them into being what it was never intended for them to be—little adults. Such parents know what to expect along the way from infancy to adulthood, and know better than to expect a child of theirs to match the scale perfectly. They have learned how to recognize and respect individual differences among their own children against the background of the maturation process. They know better than to compare. Having acquired a sufficient background of knowledge of children in general, they give themselves to the fascinating adventure of becoming acquainted with their own children in particular.

Modern parents are a little suspicious of the "good child," and not too anxious about the "wild and unruly." They like children and like to watch them grow. They do not consider children as twigs to be bent, and their parenthood is not strained with twig-bending efforts. They are more likely to think of children as little persons with whom they need a better acquaintance, and with whom they want to establish lasting friendships. They understand that friendship is one of life's most rewarding experiences, and they see that the happiest families are those in which parents and children are friends. They understand that this is not a matter of "blood relationship" but of attitudes and actions which demonstrate that little people and big people are recognized as persons whose friendship is valued and desired. They know that the same things which contribute toward friendship anywhere enrich it within the family. They are aware that whatever threatens friendship anywhere will threaten it within parent-child relationships. Because they know, they try to become more skilled in the art of friendship.

Modern parents understand that children need discipline but not dominance, and they know the difference. They realize, among their children's needs, the need of reassurance to reduce fears, and affection to encourage self-confidence. They talk with their children and play with them, too. They do not talk *to* their children and play *for* them. They give them plenty of attention but do not show them off as a means of acquiring status for themselves. They want to know their children and they want their children to know them. They are aware that it is possible for parents and children to live together twenty years and never really know each other. They try, therefore, to understand each little person in their home, not as a child in general, but as a person in particular.

When a baby is born, a father and a mother are born. As the baby grows up, the father and mother must grow up, too, in their parenthood. Growing up as persons is important because it is not likely that any parent who is not grown up as a person can help a child to grow beyond his own level of maturity. But complications can arise when a parent does not grow up as a parent. It is frustrating and it usually results in angry rebellion when a young adult has a father or a mother whose parenthood is lagging back somewhere in his adolescence. Unless the "ages and stages" of parenthood correspond reasonably well to the "ages and stages" of childhood and youth, the romance of parenthood and childhood may suffer. If we understand ourselves fairly well as parents, children in general, and our own children in particular, we may experience more of the romance involved in pioneering in modern parenthood.

We Need to Understand the Child's World of Tomorrow

The patriarchal family where father was king, mother was queen, and children were little servants, is now obsolete. Pioneers in family relationships have been trying to introduce democracy into the home. As in any period of revolution, things are a bit confusing. Sometimes the positions of various members have changed, accompanied by the illusion that democracy has been initiated, when all that has happened is that mother—or not infrequently the only child—occupies the throne. We have not yet established democracy in family life, although some families seem to be nearer to it than others. Chief among the complicating factors are our traditions. They are all geared to the autocratic family. We are having to discover what a husband and father in a democratic family is like, how a mother acts, and where the children belong in the picture.

Father was unquestioned boss in "the good old days." He occupied the throne of an economic dictatorship from whence came his power and authority. Mother had to do her manipulating behind the throne, and children were taught to perform according to adult standards of childhood. Now father is off his throne, mother is out from behind it, and the children are showing the results of any shift from one ordered life to another. Husbands and wives are trying to find out what "equality" really means.

Fathers and mothers are finding it difficult to lay the rod down and take up the principles of guidance.

Some families move more readily and easily in the direction of democracy, others lag. Some husbands and wives, distraught with confusion, regress to patriarchal relationships, only not always by common consent in the same marriage. Some parents, despairing of ever handling their children by democratic means regress to authoritarian methods. Children are frequently caught between an autocratic and a democratic parent, or become the battleground between parents and teachers when the home is authoritarian and the school more democratic.

Children used to be economic assets in the producing family, and the more children the greater the wealth. In today's consuming family children are economic liabilities. It costs about twenty thousand dollars to raise one child from infancy through college. Children used to help make soap. Now they have to be taught how to buy it and use it. Families used to manufacture their own fun and recreation, largely out of personal resources of imagination, ingenuity, and initiative. Now they must depend upon commercialized recreation offered in "magnificent, stupendous, colossal" confusion. Families used to stay home a great deal. Now they meet at home on Saturday nights to divide Dad's paycheck, or go home to wait their turn with the car.

More rapid change is occurring among the things with which we live and the standards by which we live than has occurred in the whole history of the human race. World revolution is in process, involving every phase of the life of all the people on the earth. In our country the automobile has wiped out the line of distinction between Country Bumpkin and City Slicker. Will the airplane wipe out national boundaries and racial differences for our children? Television brings world events of vital significance and beauty within the reach of parents and children, but it can also bring burlesque and crime into our living room. Problems of parenthood increase apace.

Education is being pushed to realize that emphasis is shifting, determined by the needs of today, from the priority of subject matter to the prime significance of the student as a growing social being. Reading, writing, and arithmetic may have been adequate for great-granddad's needs, but a rocket age of atomic power requires that education focus toward a religious philosophy of life upon whose values democracy is based. It must develop a citizenship capable of making a democracy function. It must help us to grow up and to become acquainted with others on this earth with whom we must get along if we are to survive.

By close inspection of our ports of entry we have protected ourselves from agricultural pest, animal disease, and human epidemic. But a city discovered that it had to be concerned with a jungle fever which developed in the body of a soldier flown in from the tropics. When airplanes come from known contamination spots they are sprayed with insecticide in flight, or before passengers are allowed to disembark after landing. But it will take an incredible amount of spraying when today's children and grandchildren begin to fly about over the face of the earth. Smallpox in a grass hut in the remote jungle will be of concern to us, wherever we live, for the sake of our own health.

Crime now presents a cosmic Frankenstein aspect with three-dimensional escape and world-wide hideouts. International gangsters, equipped with radar, TV, jet planes, and atomic power may become a menace before the nations learn how to co-operate in policing the world. Cities have torn down buildings to widen streets built for horse-and-buggy shoppers, constructed expressways and inner and outer belt lines to accommodate automobile customers. Residences have moved into the country and small shopping communities have developed. Many commuters are flying to and from their work. Present airport facilities are already obsolete when compared with planes on the drawing boards in the planning rooms of the manufacturers. Communication is instantaneous between any two points on the earth. Flight has already passed a rate of twice the speed of sound. We have released more power than that represented in all the bombs dropped by England and the United States in World War II; and the final power of the atom has not, as yet, been estimated.

Chaperonage provided a sort of protection to young people of grandfather's day. The automobile made chaperonage obsolete. The airplane is making it antique. From what source will protection be provided for our children and theirs except their own inner resources? How is the transfer of protection from parent to child made? In a world where so much emphasis is placed upon success through competition, how can we cultivate the skills needed for co-operation when survival depends upon it? After taking a look at our world as we see it, attempting to anticipate what kind of world it may become if present trends continue, what kind of men and women will be needed to cope with its problems and respond to its challenge? What must we do in the home to insure the development of such men and women? How must parenthood be related to institutions in the community that deal with children in order to join forces to this end? What kind of training do we need if we are to become parents adequate to the opportunity?

Proceeding upon the basis of the known, pushing into the potential of the unknown in parenthood today can be pioneering par excellence. Learning to understand and achieve the reduction of fear and the strengthening of faith, the control of anger and the extension of good will, the adjustments of frustrations encountered in the maturation process in ways that provide for growth according to the Divine Plan, may be the most exciting and thrilling experience in life. Here is opportunity for romance even beyond that of marriage. It is the romance of participation in the creation and development of life, from the promise toward the realization of the image of God within us.

CHAPTER TEN

Romance for the Rest of Life

When we have finished our job as parents and our children have gone out into the world on their own, we have a new opportunity to add to the romance in our marriage. Whether we can take advantage of it depends upon whether we can graduate as parents, or must pine for our children and for the satisfying feeling of being needed by them. In any event we shall probably feel some touch of nostalgia during the transition from a family marriage to a postfamily marriage. The unusually slowed pace and the almost oppressive quiet around the house contribute to a feeling of being lost. It may dawn on us then that we are free to turn toward each other more completely than at any time since the first baby was born. With resources of understanding and sympathy, patience and encouragement, and a more abundantly giving love enriched by the experiences of parenthood we may be more adequately prepared to meet each other's needs than when we were first married.

Planning Is Important

We may contribute to the romance of this "second honeymoon" time in life if we have looked ahead and made plans for it. One of our most important concerns during the postfamily years and on through the retirement years is health. As the childhood years are preparation for adult life, so the family years are preparation for the rest of life. We can safeguard our happiness as far as health is related to it by taking care of ourselves before the years when diabetes, kidney troubles, and heart diseases threaten most.

Another important matter about which we would be wise to do some planning is that of income. The economic system in our country was created by and for youth. As we grow older we cannot compete as we once did and our income is less. If we have prepared for retirement by developing some avocation to which we can switch, or by careful saving, we may be able to take care of ourselves without help. In the old days families stayed together more frequently, and the economic welfare of the aging was assured as a part of the larger family income. Today's families break up into small units, independent of the parental family and each other, and grandparents are frequently left to themselves, or become a burden for grown children, or depend upon charity. All kinds of feelings of resentment, guilt, obligation, gratitude, and conflict may develop from situations which emerge because of a lack of good planning. Foresight may help to prevent suffering.

When we are no longer tied down by our responsibilities to our children we may engage in more community life. We may take advantage of opportunities for our own personal pleasure which we had to pass up previously. We may find joy in making it possible for others to take advantage of them, too. Because of our maturity and experience we are better prepared to serve our community in some ways than when we were young. Much of the satisfaction formerly derived from our parental responsibilities may now be secured through directing our concerns more extensively toward the larger community family of which we are a part.

One Family Planned Well

Frank and Marie Jamison became aware of the need for planning as they reached the middle years. (We are not calling them by their real names.) About the time their first child entered high school, they began to plan for the years when their children would be gone. It would be six years before their youngest child would be ready for high school, so they took their time but they did not think that it was too early to start. They rechecked their insurance and reworked their savings plan, and calculated their future needs according to their best estimates. They started a travel fund and began gathering information about parts of the country which they wanted to see.

Two days after their last child was married and on her honeymoon they began to rearrange the house according to plans which they had made for the time when they would be alone again. Henceforth their children would be visitors, and only visitors' facilities would be needed. Frank began to install in the basement the power tools which he had purchased on time payments covering several months. They moved the wall from between two of the children's rooms and made a large craftshop and sewing room. Frank turned out desk and floor lamp bases, and Marie finished them and made shades for them. She painted the shades until they hit upon the idea of using photographs in shades. Then they built a darkroom and both learned photography. They spent many happy hours in the country taking pictures which they thought might make good lamp shades. They gave their first lamps as presents, but soon orders were coming in for purchase. It was not long before they were swamped with more orders than they could fill.

Frank did not retire; he quit. He had developed a way to mount color photographs on natural wood framed with bark, and in addition to the lamp work, this took so much time that he quit his former job in self-defense. He and Marie seemed to enjoy being together more than ever. Their time was their own, and they worked when they wished, stopped when they liked, and went off in their trailer frequently, usually toward fishing waters somewhere. Frank said that he had to do it to get away from people who wanted him to make something for them.

Marie pitched into community enterprises, helping out in so many "worthy causes" that she began to call herself a professional collector. She learned more about her town than all she had known while her children were growing up. She belonged to the Library Board and kept up with her work in the church. She went on business trips with Frank, a thing she could never do while the children were home. She was impatient with other women who were always complaining that they had nothing to do, or who were too ill to do anything.

When their grown children came and brought their young families it took Frank and Marie days to get the place straightened up after they were gone. There were always new tools to be bought to replace old ones which had been broken by small hands busy with hobby horses and scooters. They loved the noise of the day and the quiet evenings of talk after the little ones had been put to bed. It amused both Frank and Marie when their children began to show the sort of solicitude characteristic of the middle-aged for their aging parents. They had quite a time trying to keep their children from running their lives completely. Marie remarked that it served them right. Their children were only getting it back at them for the years during which they had run their children's lives. Frank allowed that Marie was asking for it, the way she seemed so helpless when they were around. They liked to tease each other mildly, and their sense of humor held to the end. Frank said, on the very day he died, he guessed that at last he would be free from her bossing. But Marie shook her head and said that this was one trip which she had been looking forward to making with him, and he should wait around out there. She wouldn't be very far behind.

Our Attitude Toward Ourselves Is Important

One of the strongest supports for romance in marriage through the rest of life is the feeling that we are needed and wanted by the one in the marriage with us. Our children do not need us as they once did; business and industry may turn to younger men; and unless we realize that we need each other more than ever we may suffer the aching pain of feeling unwanted. Older people used to be confronted with youths who sought counsel and advice. Now young people turn to the school, or the library, or the technical specialist for information and consultation. More than ever the younger generation is likely to look upon us as old-fashioned and out of date. We could easily begin to feel tired, and lonely, and not very important. These feelings may be warded off by people who love each other, and respect each other, and want each other.

During the retirement years, a threat rooting in an

old habit may cause us misery and pain because of the way we may come to think of ourselves. We might measure the last of life by the middle, or even the first. If we expect to be just as chipper and influential as we were in the "prime" of life we are doomed to disappointment. But we do not ordinarily think of age as having any prime. The only standard of measurement seems to be a middle-aged standard. If most of our sense of worth is tied up with a picture in our mind which represents us at our "prime," no wonder we are reluctant to tell our age after we have passed it. It becomes understandable when we brag about doing something as well as we did "when we were in our prime."

It is well enough for business and industry to work out means of using older people and thus prolong their economic value. But the greater need is for us to construct an entirely different frame of reference for measuring from that used by business and industry. There just might be values in a person's worth besides his economic productivity and his sense of status that goes with it. We shall continue to do ourselves and others grave injustice until we develop measurements appropriate to the capacities of age, and stop measuring age by the younger years. When we measure ourselves this way, particularly when our sense of worthfulness is tied too securely to the peak of our economic productivity, we are bound to conclude that we are not worth very much. Our self-respect will suffer accordingly. The married couple can counteract these feelings, to great measure, by recognizing in themselves and in each other, worthfulness of another kind altogether. They do not have to fool themselves about weaknesses and limitations imposed by age. They need only to accept these and make the most of potentialities which have emerged with age.

As we grow older, friends of long standing begin to recede beyond our reach. We move our residence, or they go to some other community, or death thins the ranks. We need them because they belong to our world, and the present world seems very different. There is no other world except ours in which we may feel at home. Friends reassure us of our importance and worth. We love to share in recollections and memories which seem to be ties that bind and hold our world together. Friends stave off loneliness. We may protect the romance in our marriage by making new friends, but of greater importance is the friendship which a husband and a wife may have for each other. Mutual experience, priceless memories, and friendship may draw a couple together in the romance of a oneness achievable only during the aging years.

This drawing together does not mean withdrawal from the life of the community, and from relationships with relatives. It means mutual support in their adventure in discovering new relationships to the community and to their kinsfolk. Grandparents may have the joys of relationships with children, without the responsibilities of parenthood. When grown children are mature enough to consult their parents about grandchildren, and grandparents are mature enough not to confuse consultation with the re-establishment of parenthood, the young parents may benefit from the wisdom of age and experience, and the aging may feel of real value in the lives of their family. One of the richest experiences of childhood is to be found in the association with grandparents who are happy and content. One of the most rewarding experiences to grandparents may be in their association with their children's children.

The peak of romance in marriage may have been reached when a couple have become so closely identified that they feel not only at one with themselves but with all other human beings on the earth. Love may become so abundant and mature that it breaks through the bonds of matrimony and encompasses men and women and children wherever there is a need for love. Sympathy and understanding, generosity and concern reach out to include the bewildered and the lonely wherever they are found. Financial means may be limited, but respect for the human spirit is boundless. Physical strength may be wavering, but faith in the fundamental goodness of man is enduring and firm. Immediate family ties may be weakened or broken, but the ties of brotherhood in the family of God are secure.

We Envy the Romance of a Mature Marriage

Most of us have somewhere run across a couple of old people who cause us to stop a moment and enjoy their company. We wish that we might be somewhat like them when we grow old. Maybe it is the way they look at each other and talk to each other. Maybe it is the way they look at us and talk with us. Anyway we suspect that they know love beyond our comprehension. As they talk we are impressed that they have come to value each other more than anything or anyone else. We feel they have grown up as well as grown old, and there is an easy grace about them which marks the difference between them and many others. There is no anxiety or fear lurking in the shadows within their eyes. They are relaxed and seemingly without tension. No criticism, or scorn, or contempt makes a jagged edge to their voice. There is no sense of loneliness or isolation. We know that they have the priceless resources of love and that they gave them to each other.

They will tell us about their children and their grandchildren, and perhaps their great-grandchildren, but they will not bore us with them. We wish we could get our hands upon some of the joy which they show while they talk. For a while we feel that we are with the happiest and the proudest people in the world, and it gives us a lift. We can see that there is nothing false in their pride, because it is in each other.

Theirs is a lifetime of developing romance. It is as extensive as the knowledge upon which they based their decisions, and by which they shaped their expectations. It is as strong as their achievements in the fine art of living together. Their romance is as beautiful as the colors of their personalities, and as clearly focused as their sense of values. It is as packed with exploration and adventure as the limits of their faith and courage. Romance has enabled them to walk the streets of the commonplace and to turn them into avenues of the unusual. It is as full of fun and excitement as their philosophy of life.

Their eyes do not seem strained from looking into the shadows of the past. They are bright with reflections of the joys cast against the possibilities of each new day. Their faces seem to be animated with the happiness of the here and now. It is clear to all their friends that they have hope enough to light a little way ahead, and faith enough to walk that far hand in hand.

We are sad when we hear that they have gone, but we are glad because we know that they have had romance enough for all their life.

CHAPTER ELEVEN

Keeping Romance in Your Marriage

Fate determines the matter of romance in your marriage, but your knowledge and understanding of romance determine your fate. Destiny decrees that you shall have romance, more or less, or not at all, but your ability to get along decides your destiny. Successful flights and happy landings are achieved by pilots who understand that these results are not due to forces over which they have no control. Romance in marriage depends upon you, and upon the person on whom you bet your life when you married.

In order to keep romance in your marriage you need to understand the difference between romance before and after a wedding. Some married people are most unhappy because they expected romance in marriage to be exactly like that with which they entered it. They are doomed to miss romance because of their own expectations. When they fell in love they were caught up and whirled upon dizzy flights of fantasy through rainbow clouds of romantic illusion. The little time which they could spend together sparked imagination and conjured up ecstatic dreams. Sex urges, which drive toward mating, are blocked for many good reasons in our society, and this restriction to marriage inflates the power of attraction just as standing in front of a closed bakery tantalizes the appetite of a hungry person and enhances the anticipation of dining.

When you married you moved into an intimacy of acquaintance which dissipated much of the dream and confronted you with a "down to earth" husband or wife. Sex hunger was satisfied. That portion of romance which depended upon dreams and the restraining of sex disappeared. The fading away of this part of premarital romance has been interpreted by many as the dying out of love and the passing of romance. For those whose only idea of romance is limited to the illusion-packed experience before a wedding, romance in marriage is meager, if they experience it at all.

You can keep romance in your marriage if you understand that what you keep is mostly what you create as you go along, and not just what you had back yonder somewhere. If you are successful in the general run of ordinary day-to-day getting along and can make your marriage a long story of love filled with enough reassurance to balance the anxiety, enough gladness to dissipate the gloom, enough excitement and thrill to counteract the drudgery and boredom, the adventure of your marriage will *be* your romance.

Your fate is a happy one if your love for your husband or wife, and the love which comes your way, is free of jealousy which characterizes childish or even adolescent love. If you find yourself always thinking about what you can do or say to make your husband or wife happy, your destiny will be full of romance because your love has grown beyond its youthful self-centeredness and you can contribute toward the fulfillment and enrichment of your loved one's life. If both of you have that sort of love for each other, you can live for each other. Romance is guaranteed with such loving and such living.

You can keep romance in your marriage if your sex life is an expression of mature love. People who love exploitatively use sex exploitatively. Some people indulge in sex for its own satisfaction, and love has nothing to do with it. If sex is sought on an animal level, nothing but animal returns can be expected. Other threats to romance, as sex is involved in it, are ignorance and unhealthy attitudes and feelings. Ideas that sex is low and beastly, vulgar and nasty and sinful will prevent adjustment according to the Creator's plan. Mix deceit and thoughtlessness, lack of respect, and sex for its own sake—and romance, if not marriage itself, may be doomed.

If this physical and spiritual relationship, which is the most intimate form of human communication there is, serves to convey love with all the finer resources of personality supporting it, a couple may know romance that would be impossible under any other circumstances. Mix with the feelings of tender affection the idea that sex is a part of God's plan, clean if we are clean; add sympathy and understanding, courtesy and trust, passion tempered with respect, and a desire that the experience may be wonderful for your loved one—and the contact of bodies may but symbolize the merging of spirits in a oneness that will color romance with rainbows and stars.

You can keep romance in your marriage if you realize that you married quite a flock of relatives along with the lucky one who married you. In all possibility you have long since discovered that these relatives do not love you in quite the same manner as the person whom you married loves you. In such a case nothing works quite so well as treating in-laws as if they were not relatives but valued friends. Some relatives are just that. But it is easy to take things for granted, and make assumptions which can be misinterpreted as taking advantage, ignoring the common courtesies and disregarding the rights of others, when no such thing is intended. We want our relatives to feel freer with us and we assume that they want us to feel free with them. The best insurance for happy relationships is in being more careful and considerate than with people in general.

Parents on either side in your marriage may scatter the makings of romance along through your marriage if they have stopped being parents. They did a good job if they brought you up to be a responsible adult who no longer needs to depend upon them to tell you what to do, when to do it, and how it should be done. If your marriage is threatened by prolonged parent-child relationships, you married too soon and still have to grow up, for you and your parents have never been weaned. In any case romance will thrive in proportion to the adult relationships in which people refrain from trying to run other people's lives for them. Wherever adults have affection which is not used to create a sense of obligation or control by dominance, in-laws may add to the tone and quality of romance in any marriage.

It takes about seven years for the average couple to learn to manage their financial affairs in such manner that money is not a big problem in their marriage. If you learned how to handle it before you married you already know how this skill supports romance. If you are having trouble, look up some financial adviser and go about the business of your marriage as a business. The chief problem seems to be management. Many people are very successful at making money, and awful failures at spending it.

Shake yourself free from traditional ideas about who makes the money, who keeps the records, and who spends the money. In nearly one-third of our families today it is the wife who manages all the money, no matter who makes it. Women do most of the buying for the modern home. Many of them are excellent bookkeepers. If tradition has dominated your ideas about who handles the money, and how, you can be miserable unless you do things as your grandparents did, but romance may be sold out if you do. You do not live in the world of your grand-parents.

Charge accounts and loans may be very helpful, but great caution must be exercised or you can get into debt over your head before you know it. Buying on the spur of the moment, by impulse, proves that it pays the dealer to study the psychology of selling, but it may give you financial hangovers, and prove that *you* need to study the psychology of buying. Love may be the most important thing in marriage, but it has to rest on a balanced budget, or it does not rest!

If your marriage is mutually satisfying you have the best insurance against the threat of the "eternal triangle." Hungry people may steal when they get hungry enough. All of us hunger for love and respect, for regard and esteem, for sympathy and understand-ing, for companionship and adventure. If married people give themselves to the satisfaction of these needs in each other's lives, the "tall, dark, and hand-some" cannot exercise quite so much mysterious power over the wife, nor can some silly, sensual wench so easily make a monkey out of the husband. But if your marriage is unsatisfying, almost any gen-eral run-of-the-mill third party may bring what ro-mance you have crashing down around your ears.

Since a wedding does not blind people, nor de-sex them, there is always the possibility of feelings of re-sponse to outside attraction somewhere along through marriage. At such times romance in marriage may depend upon the ability of the one affected to hold to commitments and carry out responsibilities assumed at the wedding. At such a point there is no substitute for character. In such a crisis people demonstrate the difference between the immature and the mature, or the animal and the human.

People who live for each other because they love each other will go out of their way to make each other happy. It is hard for any third party to make much headway in such a marriage.

When you were single you were free from the necessity of taking anyone into account as you made personal decisions. But you were barred from the joys of possessing and belonging which constitute some of the freedom of the married. When you were single you were free from the responsibilities of fidelity to any one person, except yourself, but you were blocked or else restricted to clandestine affairs. When you were single you could come and go as you liked if you lived alone, but were locked out from the experience of going home to someone who waited and longed for you and depended upon you.

When you married you exchanged certain freedoms available in single life for other freedoms available only in married life. Romance has been shattered by some who thought that they could gain the freedoms of marriage while holding on to the freedoms of single life. Romance can be increased by the abundant use of the freedoms to give unreservedly, which have been acquired through the wedding. The best way to discover such freedoms is to practice thinking and feeling, eating and sleeping with a "we" consciousness of life. It is not easy at first because most of us get pretty good at the "I" way of living before we marry. The "ball and chain" attitude of married people toward each other is a confession of failure to turn loose from the freedoms of single life, and make the most of the freedoms of marriage. Romance can be found only in those marriages with married people in them.

Emotional immaturity is the chief cause of trouble in marriage. Some people never grow up. Forty years of age, six feet in height, and 180 pounds of weight do not add up to maturity enough for marriage. A man can still lose his temper like a child, or chase some female barely out of her teens when he is old enough to be her father. A woman can force herself into clothes which she thinks make her appear young, and she can imitate the juvenile under the illusion that she is admirably gay, long after she has passed the bud stage and is in full bloom.

If your parents were not adequate in helping you to grow up or if you failed to respond to their efforts, you must still struggle for attention, strive for status, strain to insure that "what they say" is favorable, compete to achieve "success" no matter what happens to you or others in the process, fight to get your own way, storm or sulk when frustrated, or become ill, blame everybody else but yourself for mistakes and failures, play at romantic love, daydream for excitement and adventure, and otherwise demonstrate why there is no romance in your marriage.

If you suspect yourself as being somewhat immature, make sure and then work on it. Nothing pays off in so much happiness in the long run as deliberate conscious efforts to continue growing all through the years. Pick out the ways in which you think you might profit by additional growth and practice. A husband and a wife who are grown up enough to be reasonably tolerant of themselves and each other, may have enough patience to lend a hand when efforts are being made toward maturity. Such co-operation will pay off in romance.

Modern parenthood is full of the romance of pioneering. Explorations into the external universe outside man are producing miracles. But greater miracles may come from discoveries within the realm of the human spirit and its relationships. Surprising revelations have already been made with respect to parenthood. The possibilities of romance are increased in proportion to our understanding of ourselves as parents, our understanding of children in general and our own children in particular, and the world in which they must find their happiness.

Parents individually and in groups are examining the findings from research which help them to understand how they "got that way" as parents. Insights derived from such examinations help them to realize more clearly the effects of their relationships with their children. If their own experience has proved to be conducive to happiness they understand more clearly why, and are better able to insure similar experience for their children. If they discover threatening attitudes and feelings they learn how to modify them and reduce their threat to their children. The great unknowns in the realm of parenthood are being explored, and modern parents are anxious to understand themselves because of their realization of the importance of such understanding to their success as parents. It builds confidence based upon facts, by contrast to confidence based upon hearsay assumptions called "common sense."

Childhood is being explored with all the tools of modern science. The process of normal growth is becoming more clearly recognizable. Parental attitudes and actions conducive to growth are being more positively identified. "Ages and stages" are being understood sufficiently to relax parents who are free from the necessity of comparing their children with any scale. Individual differences are being recognized with a better understanding of their meaning. Slowly but surely parents are groping through the maze of confusion created by the change of concern from a pattern of performance for a child, to recognition of individual needs and their satisfaction.

You can keep romance in your marriage if you join the ranks of the investigators by participation in some group discussions where parents are trying to understand themselves better, and become better acquainted with children. New insights are emerging with reference to the maturation of parents as parents and its relationship to the rate of growth of their children. You may profit by reading or by hearing a specialist, but you are a pioneer in your efforts to foresee the kind of world in which your child will live.

The patriarchal family is giving way to the democratic family, but nobody knows just what that is like. There is the problem of learning how to treat each other as husband and wife, as well as parent and child, in this new kind of home. There is the prime problem of learning the difference between discipline and dominance, in the discharge of our parenthood. Parents concerned about romance are striving to anticipate the meaning of the airplane in the life of their child. All products of this age of miracle which will affect his life are being examined. An effort is being made to understand the sort of person who can best deal with the rocket age of atomic power in order that we may contribute most toward the development of such persons in our dealings with our children.

You can keep romance in your marriage through all the retirement years if you graduate as parents, and find out how to plan to best insure health, economic security, and the success of your postfamily marriage. Parenthood should have increased your skills of giving and further developed those personal resources which contribute most toward romance. With the discharge of the responsibilities of parenthood you may turn toward each other and express your love through respect, esteem, and encouragement more powerfully than ever. The threats of loneliness and anxiety may disappear before your friendship and companionship. Personal shortcomings and weaknesses which come along with age may be accepted and discounted by those who have learned to love.

You can keep romance in your marriage all the rest of the way through life if you adjust your attitudes toward yourself to match your "age and stage" in life. You can make yourself miserable if you must measure yourself by some standard set at the time of your peak of achievement in economic productivity or personal influence, known as the "prime" of life. You may have the rich romance of a mature marriage if you continue to extend your knowledge of yourselves and marriage, and shape your expectations accordingly. You can know romance in proportion to the development of your personalities and the sharpening of your sense of values. Faith and courage will strengthen and enhance your personalities, and a religious philosophy of life may provide assurance enough for your mutual needs. Turning toward each other, and toward the larger world of human hunger with a love capable of responding to it may color romance with indescribable hues.

The steady warm glow of romance from the past may fall over your shoulders and color the way ahead with rainbows and the promise of the greatest romance of all on into the great beyond.

IF YOU WANT TO READ FURTHER

ON MARRIAGE

Marriage for Moderns, Henry A. Bowman (New York: McGraw-Hill, 1948)

When You Marry, Evelyn M. Duvall and Reuben L. Hill (New York: Association Press, 1951)

Marriage and Family Relationships, Robert G. Foster (New York: Macmillan, 1950)

Building a Successful Marriage, Judson Taylor Landis and Mary G. Landis (New York: Prentice-Hall, 1948)

Love and Marriage, F. Alexander Magoun (New York: Harper, 1951)

Marriage, the Art of Lasting Love, David R. Mace (New York: Doubleday, 1952)

Marriage Is What You Make It, Paul Popenoe (New York: Macmillan, 1950)

ON SEX IN MARRIAGE

(See individual chapters in the books above.)

Sex Life in Marriage, Oliver M. Butterfield (New York: Emerson, 1952)

The Marriage Manual, Hannah M. Stone and

Abraham Stone (New York: Simon & Schuster, 1952)

On Maturity

Attaining Maturity, Luella Cole (New York: Farrar & Rinehart, 1944)

The Mature Mind, Harry A. Overstreet (New York: W. W. Norton, 1949)

On Parenthood

These Are Your Children, Jenkins, Schacter, and Bauer (Chicago: Scott, Foresman, 1949)

The Discipline of Well-Adjusted Children, Grace Langdon and Irving W. Stout (New York: John Day, 1952)

Their Mothers' Sons, Edward A. Strecker (Philadelphia: Lippincott, 1952)

Baby and Child Care, Benjamin Spock, M. D. (New York: Pocket Books, 1946)

Today's Children and Yesterday's Heritage, Sophia Blanche Fahs (Boston: Beacon Press, 1951)

On Finances

Managing Your Money, Lasser and Porter (New York: Henry Holt, 1953)

Consumer Problems, Arch W. Troelstrup (New York: McGraw-Hill, 1952)

The Consumer's Guide to Better Buying, Sidney Margolius (New York: New American Library, 1952)